IMAGES ACROSS THE AGES

MEXICAN PORTRAITS

Dorothy
and
Thomas Hoobler

RSVP
RAINTREE
STECK-VAUGHN
P U B L I S H E R S
The Steck-Vaughn Company

Austin, Texas

Cover and interior design: Suzanne Beck
Illustrations: Robert Kuester, Represented by Creative Freelancers
Electronic Production: Scott Melcer
Project Manager: Joyce Spicer

Library of Congress Cataloging-in-Publication Data
Hoobler, Dorothy.
 Mexican portraits / by Dorothy and Thomas Hoobler : illustrated by Robert Kuester.
  p. cm. — (Images across the ages)
 Includes bibliographical references and index.
 Summary: Presents biographical sketches of Nezahualcóyotl, Moctezuma II, Malinche, Juan Diego, Diego de la Cruz, Juana Inés de la Cruz, Father Miguel Hidalgo, Benito Juárez, Pancho Villa, Emiliano Zapata, Diego Rivera, Frida Kahlo, and Amalia Hernández.
 ISBN 0-8114-6376-1
 1. Mexico — Biography — Juvenile literature. [1. Mexico— Biography.] I. Hoobler, Thomas. II. Kuester, Robert, ill. III. Title. IV. Series: Hoobler, Dorothy. Images across the ages
CT554.366 1993
920.072—dc20   92-13642
                                                          CIP AC

Printed and bound in the United States by Lake Book, Melrose Park, IL
1 2 3 4 5 6 7 8 9 0 LB 98 97 96 95 94 93

Acknowledgments
Grateful acknowledgement is made for permission to publish the lines of poetry by Sor Juana Inés de la Cruz, from *Ten Notable Women of Latin America*, by James and Linda Henderson, published by Nelson-Hall, 1978. Our thanks to Armando Olea for his help and advice.

CONTENTS

INTRODUCTION

THE EAGLE AND THE CACTUS

Nearly a thousand years ago, a band of people called Aztecs left Aztlan, their homeland somewhere in the north of Mexico. They brought with them their Nahuatl language ("the pleasant tongue") and a strong will to succeed. In an ark of reeds, four priests carried their god Huitzilopochtli [wee-tseel-oh-POK-tlee]—the Blue Hummingbird of the South. The Hummingbird was a god of war who could predict the future through the dreams of the priests. As the Aztecs journeyed south, the god gave the people a new name. "Now you shall not call yourselves Aztecs any more, now you are Mexicas." (The Mexica gave their name to the modern nation of Mexico. However, we will continue to refer to them as Aztecs to distinguish them from the other people living in Mexico at that time.)

The Aztecs suffered great hardships in their wanderings. They hunted deer, rabbits, birds, and snakes for food. Often they were hungry and thirsty and almost naked. What kept them going were Huitzilopochtli's assurances that he had chosen them to be a special people. He promised, "I will make you lords and kings of all that is in the world."

After about 200 years, the Aztecs arrived at the Valley of Mexico, a high plateau surrounded by volcanic mountains. Spread over much of the floor of the valley was Lake Texcoco. Small kingdoms around its shores competed for power. The people of these kingdoms scorned the newcomers, calling them "the people whose face nobody knows." The Aztecs had to fight to find a place for themselves.

Attacked by their enemies and seemingly facing defeat, the Aztecs drew hope from a prophecy. The priests announced that Huitzilopochtli foresaw that they would build a great city. The god told them to look for a large and beautiful cactus. They would see an eagle perching on it, holding a snake in its beak.

The very next day, the struggling Aztecs found the cactus, just as it had been described. Overcome with joy, they knelt before the cactus as if it were a divine being. At last the wanderers had a home, on an island three miles from the shoreline of Lake Texcoco. On this spot the Aztecs built their city, calling it Tenochtitlán [tuh-nok-tee-TLAN], the Place of the Cactus. The eagle, perched on a cactus with a snake in its beak, is today the national emblem of Mexico.

The Aztecs were latecomers in Mexico. When they arrived, they did not know the skills of farming. But they were heirs to a great tradition of culture stretching back 2,000 years. Earlier Mexican civilizations, the Olmec, Maya, and Toltec, had built empires based on the cultivation of corn, squash, and beans. These earlier peoples built massive pyramids and created elaborate sculptures. Through their knowledge of astronomy and mathematics, the Maya developed the most accurate calendar devised by any ancient people. The Aztecs learned from the achievements of their predecessors and became part of the broader native Mexican culture.

In the same way, modern Mexico is a blend of the ancient native cultures plus the influence of 300 years of Spanish rule. In today's Mexico City, the Plaza of the Three Cultures symbolizes the different elements of Mexican history. Surrounding the square are the remains of an Aztec pyramid, a colonial-era Catholic church, and a modern skyscraper. These pre-Columbian, colonial, and modern influences are visible everywhere in Mexico. On October 12, Columbus Day in the United States, Mexicans observe the Day of the Race. It celebrates the rich and diverse heritage of the Mexican people. "The history of Mexico," according to Octavio Paz, the nation's greatest poet, "is the history of a man seeking his parentage."

FASTING COYOTE—
NEZAHUALCÓYOTL

Nezahualcóyotl was scared. The sixteen-year-old boy and his father, the king of Texcoco, hid in a rocky ravine with a few faithful warriors. They had been driven out of their kingdom on the shore of Lake Texcoco by invaders from Azcapotzalco, the strongest power in the Valley of Mexico.

A messenger came to warn them that some traitors had revealed their hiding place. The king turned to Nezahualcóyotl and urged him to hide in a grove of trees. Facing certain death, the king wanted his son to survive and some day regain control of the kingdom.

"My dearly loved son, lion's arm, Nezahualcóyotl," he said, "I am forced to depart from this life. I beg and charge you not to forsake your subjects... to recover your empire... and to avenge the death of your afflicted father. You will make use of bow and arrow. Now you must simply hide in this grove, because your innocent death would bring to an end the very ancient empire of our ancestors."

Nezahualcóyotl watched helplessly from a nearby tree as enemy warriors approached. Soon obsidian knives flashed in the sunlight, and the young man saw his father slain. The king was stripped of his cotton armor and his body left to rot. Still hiding, Nezahualcóyotl saw a new group of men approach, but they were loyal subjects of the dead king. They took his body and dressed it in the blue royal regalia and made a chair to place him on before they lit a huge bonfire to cremate the body.

With relief, Nezahualcóyotl approached his countrymen. He prayed over the body of his father and vowed that he would return and take back his kingdom. He told his faithful subjects to return home and pretend to be loyal to the new rulers. He promised that

he would come back some day. But now he was weak and had to avoid the clutches of his enemies.

For the next few years he lived as his name foretold. In the Nahuatl language, Nezahualcóyotl means "Fasting Coyote." He would go hungry and live in fear of discovery, but in the end he would prevail.

Nezahualcóyotl was born in 1402, the son of King Ixtlilxochitl and a princess from Tenochtitlán. Almost from birth, the youngster was cared for by a gentle philosopher who guided his education. He learned the glyphs, the symbols that enabled him to read the bark or deerskin books of ancient Mexico. Early on, Fasting Coyote showed a love of poetry and learning.

Then at age twelve, he entered the *calmecac*, the special school for the sons of the nobility. It trained those who would rule or fight—the lords, lawmakers, and captains of war. Nezahualcóyotl learned about all the gods and the laws of Texcoco. He also trained in the techniques of combat. Although he was the king's son, he was treated no differently from other students. The school was tough. When Nezahualcóyotl enrolled, his philosopher-teacher warned, "Here you see the house where your father and mother offered you, the house of weeping and sadness, where those that are trained are worked like precious stones."

The students' only meals consisted of water and tortilla, the corn wafer. Each night Nezahualcóyotl was required to perform a "night journey" to test his humility and courage. He walked alone, naked and shivering, playing a shell horn and holding the sharp points of the maguey cactus. After piercing his tongue with a spike, he left the bloody thorn as an offering. In Texcoco, as in the rest of early Mexico, suffering was a necessary part of life. After a little sleep on a thin mat, he was awakened for a cold bath. But he rose quickly. The punishment for laziness was to be pricked all over with thorns.

While Nezahualcóyotl was at the calmecac, tensions increased between Texcoco and the neighboring kingdom of Azcapotzalco. Tezozomoc, the aggressive and cruel ruler of Azcapotzalco, was the most powerful king in the Valley of Mexico. He wanted to extend his control over every kingdom in the area.

As an insult, Tezozomoc sent cotton to Texcoco. He demanded

that it be woven into fine cloaks to show that Texcoco was just a tribute-paying state. But King Ixtlilxochitl refused. "Out of your cotton we will make quilted cotton armor that even your obsidian points cannot pierce," he responded. This meant war.

At first Texcoco's warriors were successful in battles with Tezozomoc's forces. Then Tezozomoc used trickery. He asked Ixtlilxochitl to meet him in friendship. Suspecting a trick, the Texcoco ruler sent one of his sons instead. Tezozomoc captured the son and flayed him alive, spreading his skin on a rock on the road. He then moved against the city of Texcoco.

Though Ixtlilxochitl and his soldiers fought bravely, Tezozomoc's forces were too powerful. The people of Texcoco fled the doomed city. At last the king abandoned it too, taking his son and a few faithful followers. Ixtlilxochitl soon met his terrible fate.

The sixteen-year-old Fasting Coyote now began a time of wandering. He knew that Tezozomoc would pursue him, but the young man used the skills learned in the calmecac to survive. He traveled beyond the volcanoes to seek allies and safety. Then he returned to the Valley, eluding Tezozomoc at every turn. People began to tell stories of his exploits. Fasting Coyote gained the reputation of being a magician who was favored by the gods.

Fasting Coyote realized that he needed help to regain his throne. He went to Tenochtitlán and suggested to the Aztecs that they unite with him and another city in a Triple Alliance to defeat Azcapotzalco. Their task was made easier by the death of Tezozomoc. His successor lacked the former leader's military skills.

Nezahualcóyotl assembled an army of followers who still regarded him as the ruler of Texcoco. He ordered his men to cast off the colorful feathers and jewels that Mexican warriors traditionally wore for battle. They should wear only white cotton cloaks.

His men were disturbed by the order, but Nezahualcóyotl drew them together and told them, "It seems as if I were in a garden filled with a variety of flowers, and in which you, the fragrant blossoms of the jasmine, with no more adornment than a simple whiteness, are supreme among the blooms." He felt that precious jewels and feathers did not increase their ability to fight, but merely attracted the attention of enemies who wanted to strip them of their finery.

The Triple Alliance was successful. It destroyed the city-kingdom of Azcapotzalco. Nezahualcóyotl personally slew the king, who had hidden in his steam bath. His father's death had been avenged.

After Fasting Coyote regained the throne of Texcoco, he ruled for more than forty years. His years of wandering and hardship made him more sensitive to the sufferings of his subjects. According to a chronicle, "He was a pious man with the poor, the sick, widows and the aged, and much of his rents he spent in feeding and clothing the needy, especially in years of famine.... in such years he would never sit down to eat until all the poor had been fed."

Previously, Texcoco's laws had always laid down harsh punishments for anyone who took corn from another's field. Stealing as little as seven ears meant death. But during Fasting Coyote's years of wandering he sometimes had resorted to theft to stay alive. He knew what hunger could drive a man to do. So when he became king, he ordered corn to be planted along the roads. Anyone who was in need could pick it.

The word of Nezahualcóyotl's abilities spread throughout the Valley of Mexico. In 1449 heavy rains caused Lake Texcoco to overflow its banks and flood the city of Tenochtitlán. The ruler of Tenochtitlán, Moctezuma I, turned for help to the King of Texcoco. Nezahualcóyotl designed a dike that protected the city and separated the brackish salty water from the pure water. More than nine miles long, the dike was of rock supported by timber and sand. Nezahualcóyotl's dike brought the ruler further fame.

He was a great builder at home, too. He designed a magnificent palace of great splendor. It had three hundred rooms set around courtyards and gardens. Inside the great council chamber stood the king's throne of gold encrusted with turquoise. In the hall of judgment, Nezahualcóyotl dispensed justice to his subjects. The palace included quarters for the soldiers of the guard and storage rooms to hold the tribute from neighboring cities.

The palace had a special patio that was used as a forum for poets, philosophers, and historians. Here they taught and exchanged ideas with thinkers from all over the valley. Texcoco became the center for studies of Nahuatl literature.

Nezahualcóyotl himself loved to compose poems and encouraged other poets. He often held poetry contests in which each writer sang his work to the accompaniment of a drum. To the winner,

Nezahualcóyotl presented a precious piece of jade. The second-prize winner received gold, and precious feathers went to the third-place finishers. All the contestants were awarded finely woven blankets. Sometimes the king would chant one of his own poems, like the following:

> My flowers shall not cease to live;
> my songs shall never end:
> I, the singer, intone them;
> they become scattered, they are spread about.

Nezahualcóyotl loved nature. The royal palace complex was surrounded by gardens where flowers and trees from all over the Valley were planted. To water them, he ordered the construction of special canals. Only the ruler was permitted to bathe in these waterways. A zoo was built for wild animals, as well as a bird sanctuary where Nezahualcóyotl liked to walk and enjoy the songs of nature.

Nezahualcóyotl was also fascinated by religion. From his youth, he had studied the lore of the ancient Mexican gods. During years of flooding and famine in the Valley, his allies the Aztecs made human sacrifices to regain the favor of the gods. At the urging of Moctezuma I, Nezahualcóyotl built a temple to Huitzilopochtli, but he did not approve of the mass human sacrifices offered by the Aztecs.

His study of religion brought him to the idea of a god that was powerful over all others. He called this spirit "The Lord of the Everywhere." In the temple honoring his god, there was no image. Nezahualcóyotl believed that this god had no single home but was everywhere. He expressed the idea in this poem:

> God, our Lord, is invoked everywhere.
> Everywhere is He venerated.
> It is He who creates things,
> He creates himself: God.

As Nezahualcóyotl aged, he was carried everywhere in a special chair woven of reeds. In winter he was wrapped in a cocoon of cotton and wool. Still he continued to exercise firm control over his kingdom. He began to worry about the growing power of Tenochtitlán. Although Nezahualcóyotl had created the Triple Alliance, the Aztecs had benefited from it more than their allies. They followed up their victory by making war on other neighbors, spreading their territory from the island-city to the mainland.

The old king decided that the best person to succeed him was his youngest son, Nezahualpilli. When he lay dying in 1472, he called his son and a few trusted advisers to his bedside. He warned them to beware of the Aztecs, and urged his son to follow his example of kind and wise rule. Then he sent them away so that he could die alone with his thoughts.

When Nezahualcóyotl felt death coming near, he wrote a last poem:

> I, Nezahualcóyotl, ask myself
> If perchance we take root in the earth:
> We are not here for always,
> But only tarry for a short while.
> Though it be of jade it will be shattered,
> Though it be of gold it will break,
> Though it be of quetzal feathers it will come apart.
> Nothing lasts for ever on this earth,
> But is only here for a little.

The Fasting Coyote left a legacy of poetry, architecture, engineering, and religious thought. Unfortunately, only a few of his works survive. A statue of him stands in the Texcoco of today, and a few ruins of his buildings still remain. He was the greatest of the kings of early Mexico—a genius in many fields. His poems are the earliest Mexican literature that still exists.

CHAPTER 2

THE FEARFUL RULER—
MOCTEZUMA II

A worried Moctezuma II, the Aztec ruler, walked up the 114 steps of the great pyramid temple in Tenochtitlán. He entered the darkened chamber of the house of the Blue Hummingbird. Shadows flickered on the wall, and the dim light revealed a hideous image of Huitzilopochtli. The chamber reeked of blood and gore. Around the neck of the grotesque god hung human hearts and heads. From his face, monstrous eyes stared out, embodying all the nightmares of the Aztec people.

A human victim lay spread-eagled on a stone altar. As Moctezuma watched, a black-robed priest with gore-matted hair raised his obsidian knife. He plunged it into the victim's chest. The priest reached inside and plucked out the still-beating heart. He held it aloft in triumph as an offering to the god. The body was thrown from the top of the pyramid.

Later the body would be cut into pieces. The head, along with those of many other victims, was displayed outside the temple. The torso was fed to wild animals kept in a zoo on the grounds of Moctezuma's palace. The arms and legs were cooked and eaten at a ritual meal by the worshipers of Huitzilopochtli.

Moctezuma, like all his people, believed that these bloody rituals were necessary to save the universe. To the Aztecs, human sacrifice ensured that the sun would rise each morning and cross the sky, bringing its warmth and light to the cornfields.

Before the sun appeared in the morning sky, the Aztecs observed that the sky turned pink and then red. They believed that it was blood that propelled the sun upward. As the chosen people of Huitzilopochtli, they had the duty to supply human blood to keep the sun moving. Every day at dawn, Aztec priests sacrificed a new victim to ensure that the greatest disaster they could imagine—the death of the sun—would not occur.

13

Whenever the gods showed their displeasure, the Aztecs increased their sacrifices. Besides, Moctezuma's empire, which now spread from the Caribbean Sea to the Pacific Ocean, had suffered several years of hardship. Rainfall had been sparse and the crops had failed. His subjects were restless and unhappy. Moctezuma desperately hoped to appease the gods and regain their favor. He ordered his warriors to capture, rather than kill, their enemies so they could be used as sacrifices. The towns of subject peoples within his domain were required to supply other victims. Even Aztecs themselves—men, women, and children—could be chosen to mount the steps of the pyramid and be offered to the hummingbird god.

When Moctezuma was born in 1467, the sound of flutes and singing came from the doorway of his father's palace. Four days later, two warriors with painted faces and feathered shields brought four young boys to the palace. These children would have the honor of performing the naming ceremony for the new child. Four times they ran around the baby, who lay on a thick cotton cloth. At each of the four cardinal directions, they stopped to call out his name and birth date. The name was Moctezuma, meaning "Angry Young Lord." The date was the year Reed One.

In a small temple across the courtyard, priests consulted the picture-writing in their books of magic. The chief priest wore the high hat and red, black, and blue costume of Quetzalcoatl, the serpent-bird god. For the year Reed One was dedicated to this god of wisdom who had brought corn and learning to the Mexican people.

The priests foretold a bright future for the infant, predicting that he would be a ruler of great wisdom. The guests sat down to a banquet of tortillas dipped in honey, fresh fruit, and other delicacies.

As the young Moctezuma grew up, he gloried in the tales of the brave Aztec warriors, and learned the names of the many gods who determined the fate of his people. He loved to walk around Tenochtitlán, which was by now a large city of about 100,000 people. Across the four broad causeways that connected it to the mainland came jade, cocoa beans, turquoise, gold, obsidian, and rare feathers as tribute from kingdoms the Aztecs had conquered.

Like Nezahualcóyotl, Moctezuma entered the calmecac and studied the sacred scripts. Moctezuma was deeply influenced by the lore of his people and took his priestly duties seriously. He especially devoted himself to the Aztec god Quetzalcoatl.

Quetzalcoatl was, in human form, a legendary ruler who had been forced to flee his kingdom. This white-skinned, bearded king sailed eastward across the great ocean. But before leaving he promised to return to regain his throne in the year Reed One.

The Aztec calendar had fifty-two years that recurred over and over in an endless cycle. The next Reed One year would come when Moctezuma was fifty-two years old, in the year 1519 in our calendar. It would be a fateful date, but to the young Moctezuma it seemed far off.

He excelled at the military arts—learning to jump with agility, withstand pain without crying out, and fight with club and spear. Growing to adulthood, Moctezuma lived up to his name. He gained a reputation as a good soldier, personally taking many prisoners. Over the years his reputation for wisdom and strength brought him respect as a leader.

In 1502 Moctezuma was chosen as Great Speaker, the Aztec title for their ruler. At his enthronement ceremony, he donned a blue war jacket and gold leggings. Ocelot-fur sandals were placed on his feet. Priests pierced his nose and placed in it a bone with hummingbird feathers. The crystal lip ornament that he had earlier worn was replaced with a blue kingfisher feather. He was then placed on his wicker throne and paraded through the streets of Tenochtitlán to the acclaim of his people.

Moctezuma, now thirty-five years old, continued the Aztec conquests, personally leading the army in some of the campaigns. Each year the Aztec empire grew, and the tribute from subject peoples increased.

Yet Moctezuma did not seem satisfied. He pored over the books of magic, asking himself whether he was doing enough to satisfy the gods. Suddenly, it seemed he was not. For Moctezuma's messengers began to bring him rumors of strange, disturbing events. A statue of Quetzalcoatl had begun to speak. It prophesied that Moctezuma would be overthrown by strangers from across the ocean.

Moctezuma turned for advice to Nezahualpilli, the son of Nezahualcóyotl. The new king of Texcoco had successfully kept the Aztecs at bay, in part because Nezahualpilli was said to be close to the gods. Moctezuma respected his ability as a forecaster and asked for a reading of the future. The answer was not reassuring. Nezahualpilli said, "I have seen with utmost certainty that within a very few years our cities are to be destroyed and laid waste."

As proof that his prophecy was true, he foretold that the Aztecs would never again win a "Flower War." The Flower Wars were battles in which the losers became sacrificial victims to the fierce Aztec gods. To prove the prophet was wrong, Moctezuma started a Flower War with Tlaxcala, a neighboring state. When news of the defeat of his warriors reached Moctezuma, he was stunned. This was the first time in history that the Aztecs had lost.

Months later, a servant in the temple of the hummingbird god saw a strange light rising in the eastern sky. The next evening, Moctezuma watched with dread to see if the report was true. About midnight he saw the long stream of light appear. The mysterious light was a comet that remained visible for forty days.

Moctezuma wept at the thought of his future. He called on the gods:

> O Lord of all creation. O almighty gods in whose hands lies the power of life and death over mortals. How can you permit that... it should fall to my lot to witness the terrible destruction of Mexico, and that I should suffer the death of my wives and children?... What shall I do? Where shall I hide?... Oh, if only I could now turn to stone, or wood, or some other form of matter, before seeing that which I now await with such dread.

In his heart, Moctezuma was ready to surrender. All that awaited was the appearance of his conqueror. That was not long in coming.

As the year Reed One approached, more frightening rumors were brought to Moctezuma. In 1517 he heard that white-skinned people, riding "temples in the sea," had landed on Mexico's east coast. Stories spread that the visitors had "fire-breathing" weapons.

White-skinned people! Moctezuma feared that this must be the return of Quetzalcoatl. He sent five of his most trusted advisers to the coast to investigate. They returned with news that frightened Moctezuma even more. The white-skinned people had a cannon that belched fire, and strange beasts the Aztecs called "stags":

> The stags came forward, carrying the soldiers on their backs.... They make a loud noise when they run... as if stones were raining on the earth. Then the ground is pitted and

scarred where they set down their hooves. It opens wherever their hooves touch it.

This was the first time Aztecs had seen horses. When Moctezuma heard the report, he felt "as if his heart shriveled." He decided to try to appease the mysterious people. He sent another delegation to the coast, this time bringing victims to be sacrificed before the visitors. When the Aztecs arrived, they set out a feast of corn, tamales, tortillas, turkey, and fruit of many kinds. The Spaniards accepted the meal gratefully. But when the Aztecs sacrificed one of their own people and offered the body to the Spaniards, the visitors rejected it with disgust.

Returning to Tenochtitlán, the delegation reported that their offering had been spurned. Worse, the white-skinned people had begun marching inland, headed for Tenochtitlán. Moctezuma was terrified; he could not decide what to do—attack the strangers or welcome them as he should if Quetzalcoatl were among them.

The Chief Speaker's brother did not share his doubts. He did not believe that these strangers were gods; they were enemies who should be fought and destroyed. But Moctezuma overruled him. He did not attack.

On November 8, 1519, the strangers reached the city. Moctezuma went to meet them at the far end of the main causeway that had been built over the water. He saw at the head of the group a small man in his early forties—Hernán Cortés. Cortés was dressed in black and projected the pride and courage of a Spanish nobleman. Moctezuma saw a determined and forceful man who would let nothing stand in his way.

A Spaniard described the meeting from the other side:

> Moctezuma descended from his litter while these great chiefs supported him with their arms beneath a marvelously rich canopy of green feathers, worked with gold and silver, pearls which hung from a kind of border that was wonderful to see. He was richly dressed and wore shoes like sandals, with soles of gold covered with precious stones.

Cortés leaped from his horse to greet the Aztec king. Moctezuma welcomed him to the city: "O Lord, our Lord, you have arrived in this land, your land, your own city of Mexico, to take possession of your throne." Moctezuma had made up his mind. Quetzalcoatl had returned.

18

The Spaniards wondered at the beauty and size of Tenochtitlán. In his letters to the Spanish king, Cortés compared the Aztec capital favorably to European cities of the time. As in Venice, many of the main thoroughfares were canals filled with small boats. Moctezuma took Cortés to the top of the pyramid and brought him inside the hummingbird's temple. The Spaniard was revolted by the sight of human sacrifice.

Cortés feared for the safety of his men. There were only 600 of them, along with anti-Aztec allies who had joined them on their march inland. He decided to ensure their safety by taking the Aztec ruler as a hostage.

Cortés led his men to Moctezuma's palace and made him a prisoner. The Chief Speaker was allowed to keep his servants and four wives and the Spaniards treated him courteously. Nevertheless, the Spaniards took over the king's palace.

Cortés' men marveled at the splendor they found within the palace, and launched expeditions to find the sources of Moctezuma's treasures of gold and silver. They wondered at his lavish life style. He ate alone, separated by a screen from his retainers. At each meal he was offered at least thirty dishes—turkey, quail, fresh fish carried over the mountains from the sea, and fresh fruits and vegetables. After his meal the screen was removed and he was served his favorite drink, *chocalatl*—made from a concoction of cocoa beans, honey, vanilla beans, and spices mixed in hot water.

After he became a prisoner, Moctezuma lost all his vitality. He became listless and unconcerned about his own fate. Despite all his efforts, all the sacrifices of blood, the gods had deserted him. He realized that Cortés was not Quetzalcoatl, but now it was too late for action.

When Cortés had to leave the capital to put down a Spanish rebellion on the coast, he left Moctezuma in the care of a subordinate. During Cortés' absence, an Aztec celebration frightened the remaining Spaniards. They opened fire on the crowd and massacred hundreds of people.

Moctezuma's brother had never shared his fear of the Spaniards. Now he organized the Aztecs in the city and surrounded the palace. The Spanish shut the doors and waited for Cortés. Moctezuma still remained helpless and passive.

Cortés, hearing of the uprising, rushed back to Tenochtitlán.

He begged Moctezuma to tell his people to stop the siege. At first the king refused. He told Cortés that he had lost the favor of the gods; he was now only an ordinary man whom no one would obey.

Finally, Moctezuma put on his turquoise-studded cloak and crown for the last time. He stepped onto a balcony of the palace where the people could see him. A hush fell over the crowd. Then voices began to cry, "Traitor!" "Coward!" Stones flew through the air. Moctezuma's crown was knocked from his head. His head bleeding, he fell to the stone floor.

There are two versions of what happened next. The Spaniards said they bandaged Moctezuma's wounds and gave him medicine. But Moctezuma pulled off the bandages. He would not eat or drink. He sat in his room for three days and then died. According to the Spaniards, his body was given to his brother. The Aztecs, however, said that Moctezuma's body was thrown out of a doorway in the middle of the night. It had been stabbed with knives.

Moctezuma's people placed his body on a funeral pyre made of wooden darts and spears. When the fire was lit, his body burst open, and clouds of black smoke poured out. The ashes were buried in an unmarked spot. It was not long before the prophecy Moctezuma feared so much would come true. Within two years, the Spaniards built their own capital on the ruins of Tenochtitlán.

CHAPTER 3

HEROINE OR TRAITOR?— MALINCHE

In early 1519 a teen-age slave girl was working in the hot low country near the Gulf of Mexico in today's state of Tabasco. Her name was Malinali, meaning "Princess of Suffering." Malinali's days were filled with drudgery and toil. She spent hours grinding corn for tortillas, sewing clothes with a cactus spine, and tending the younger children. The many religious holidays in the Aztec calendar brought even greater work. Then she had to prepare elaborate food and embroider new clothing with fancy feathers.

Still the tall girl with straight black hair and fine, regular features did not complain. She went about her tasks with quickness and efficiency. She knew that a disobedient slave could be turned over to agents from Tenochtitlán. These servants of Moctezuma collected people from all the towns under Aztec control to sacrifice to the ever-hungry gods.

In March, word came of strange boats landing on the coast to the south. The Tabascans gathered warriors to defend their towns. But the enemy was armed with powerful weapons and rode on frightening creatures that no Tabascan had ever seen before. Some even reported that the strangers and their steeds were one animal, like the mythical beast we know as a centaur.

Although the Tabascans outnumbered their foes, they feared that they might be fighting gods. Therefore, the caciques, or chiefs, gathered gifts such as fine quilted cotton and gold ornaments to please the alien Spaniards. In addition, they offered twenty slave women to cook and care for the visitors. One of these slaves was Malinali. When she entered the Spanish camp, Malinali stepped into history.

Malinali had not always been a slave. Indeed, she was born a princess in a town about two hundred miles east of Tenochtitlán.

Her father was a cacique and because of Malinali's high birth, she received a good education. As a small child, Malinali could look forward to a life of luxury. But then her father died and her mother remarried. After her mother gave birth to a son, she sought only his advancement. She saw Malinali as an obstacle to his success and sold her to a neighboring people.

Soon after, Malinali was sold again to the Tabascans. Her years in Tabasco were not wasted, however. She picked up the ability to speak a Maya dialect. That, together with her native language of Nahuatl, later enabled her to act as a translator for the Spaniards.

Despite her fears of the strange horses, ferocious dogs, and mysterious godlike men, Malinali kept her confidence. Her quick intelligence and dignified looks set her apart from the other slaves. A Spaniard named Aguilar could speak Mayan because he had been shipwrecked off the coast some years earlier. He told the slaves that the leader of the Spaniards was named Cortés and that they would be given to his leading captains. Malinali was made the servant of one of Cortés' friends.

The following day, Cortés assembled the women in front of a large wooden cross. Through Aguilar, he told them that they would receive instruction in the Christian religion. Father Olmedo, barefoot and simply dressed, taught them Catholicism. A short time later, Malinali was baptized, becoming the first Mexican Christian. She now was called Doña Marina by the Spaniards; her Christian name was pronounced Malinche by the Indians.

Soon after, she set sail with the Spaniards up the coast of Mexico. When they dropped anchor farther north, a canoe approached the ship. The Indians paddling it spoke out in the Nahuatl language. Doña Marina recognized her native tongue and soon she was translating through Aguilar to the mighty Cortés himself.

Cortés immediately saw Marina's value. He called her aside and promised that if she would translate truthfully he would protect her. From this time forward, she was constantly at Cortés' side. Soon she picked up Spanish and Aguilar was no longer necessary.

Marina was absolutely crucial to the success of Cortés. It was through her translations that he learned that many Indians resented the dominance of Moctezuma and Tenochtitlán. He realized that he could use this hostility to increase the power of his small military force. As the Spaniards marched toward Tenochtitlán, Marina's special position with Cortés did not go unrecognized by the Indians. She was known as Cortés's tongue. Her status was so high that the pair came to be called by the same name, Malintzin. This was a combination of her Christian name Marina and *tzin*, a title of respect that was added to a noble name. In the view of the Indians, they functioned as one person.

Marina proved her loyalty to Cortés at Cholula. When the Spanish soldiers entered the city, the people greeted them with friendship. But Marina sensed that something was wrong. She saw trenches dug in the street and large stew pots with chilies and tomatoes. She realized that the Cholulans were preparing to sacrifice and eat the Spaniards.

An old woman warned Marina that she should leave the city

to avoid being killed with the Spaniards. The woman offered to protect Marina in the safety of her home. She even offered her noble son as Marina's husband. After thanking her, Marina promised to return after she packed her clothes and jewels. Instead she hurried to Cortés and told him of the plot. This cemented the relationship between them. Doña Marina became Cortés' mistress as well as translator. As you read in Chapter 2, he moved on to Tenochtitlán.

Later, after Moctezuma's death, the Aztecs at Tenochtitlán attacked the Spaniards with renewed vigor. Marina remained at Cortés' side inside the palace. No longer afraid of the Spaniards' horses and guns, the Aztecs surrounded the palace. Soon the Spaniards' food and water began to run out. By July 1520 Cortés decided that he had to retreat from Tenochtitlán.

Under cover of darkness, the Spanish tried to sneak out of the city. But an Aztec sentry spotted them on the causeway, and a bloody battle followed. The Spaniards, laden down with the treasure they had looted, had to hack their way through the Aztec warriors. Many fell on both sides. Marina escaped unharmed, but she saw Cortés weep at the slaughter of so many of his men. Spanish chroniclers called the disaster the *Noche Triste*, or Sad Night.

Cortés did not want to give up his dream of conquest and glory. With Marina's help, he gathered more dissatisfied Indians to his side. Cortés assembled his new army outside Tenochtitlán early in 1521. The new Great Speaker of the Aztecs, Cuauhtémoc, put up a fierce defense. In May the Spaniards cut the aqueduct carrying fresh water to the city and began a siege. Cortés built boats to maneuver in the canals around the city.

Cut off from the mainland, Tenochtitlán's food supply dwindled. Within the city, people ate weeds, tree bark, and scum from the lake. The Aztecs began to fall ill from diseases brought by the Spaniards, such as smallpox, against which they had no immunity. Day by day, more people succumbed to starvation and illness. On August 13 the Spaniards captured Cuauhtémoc, and the starving city surrendered. An anonymous Aztec poet captured the despair of the defeat:

> Broken spears lie in the roads;
> we have torn our hair in our grief.
> The houses are roofless now, and their walls
> are red with blood....

We have chewed dry twigs and salt grasses;
we have filled our mouths with dust and bits of adobe;
we have eaten lizards, rats and worms.

Sometime after the fall of the city, Marina gave birth to Cortés' son. She named him Martin after the Spaniard's father. He was one of Mexico's first *mestizos*, or children of Spanish and Indian parents. However, after his birth the intimate relationship between the two ended when Cortés' Spanish wife arrived from Cuba.

Doña Marina was granted land and wealth to ensure her a comfortable life. However, she once again acted as a translator when, in 1526, Cortés went to Honduras to put down a rebellion. Cortés took along his captive Cuauhtémoc, who was destined to be the last Great Speaker of the Aztecs. So that the Aztecs would have no one to rally around, Cortés had him killed during this trip.

As the group traveled south, they came to the area in which Marina was born and grew up. When Cortés called for the local chiefs to come forward, Marina met her mother and half-brother. They feared she would seek revenge for her earlier mistreatment. But Marina had forgiven her mother and now embraced her. After the expedition to Honduras, Marina is lost to history.

The place where the Spaniards captured Cuauhtémoc is today the site of the Plaza of the Three Cultures in Mexico City. A plaque on the spot describes the significance of the event: "It was neither a triumph nor defeat: it was the painful birth of the mestizo nation that is Mexico today."

More than four centuries later, the Spanish Conquest still arouses controversy in Mexico. For years, not one statue of Cortés could be found in the whole country. Modern Mexico took the defeated Cuauhtémoc as its hero. In the recent years, however, Mexican President José López-Portillo, proud of his Spanish ancestry, unveiled a bust of the Spanish conquistador. López-Portillo's successor ordered it taken down.

Malinche is even more unpopular. She is the most controversial woman in Mexican history. During the three hundred years when Spain ruled Mexico, she was admired for her conversion to Christianity and her aid to Cortés. But in modern Mexico, Malinche is seen as a traitor to her people. The term *malinchism* today is one of contempt. It refers to the practice of preferring foreign things to Mexican things.

C H A P T E R 4

A Vision of the Virgin— Juan Diego

In the early morning hours of December 9, 1531, Juan Diego was making his way to the new Mexico City to attend Mass and to do his marketing. Juan Diego was an Aztec who had recently converted to Christianity. His walk to the city took him past Tepeyac Hill. Suddenly he heard the sound of singing voices coming from the top of the hill. As he listened in astonishment the music stopped, yet the whole countryside seemed to echo with the song. Then a voice called to him: "Juanito, Little Diego."

He climbed the hill and at the top he saw a lady. She beckoned him to come closer. "Juanito, the smallest of my sons, where are you going?" she asked. Juan realized that the lady before him was a holy woman. He responded, "I have to go to Your House in Mexico."

She told him, "Know and understand thou, the smallest of my sons, that I am the ever Virgin Mary, Mother of the Living God, for whom we live, of the Creator in whom everything is, Lord of Heaven and Earth." She told Juan that she wished a church to be built for her on this hill. She promised that she would "give all my love, compassion, aid, and defense because I am your Mother. To you, and all of you who invoke and trust in me." Juan promised that he would go to the Catholic bishop in Mexico City and give him the message.

Juan Diego was an Aztec born in 1474. His Nahuatl name was Quauhtlatoatzin, which means "one who talks like an eagle." Before the Spanish Conquest, he was known for his piety. Many times he made pilgrimages to Aztec religious temples and performed acts of devotion. His neighbors were in awe of his solitary mystical character. Often, Juan spent days without speaking, seeming to communicate with higher spirits.

One of the first goals of the Spanish conquerors was to convert the people of their colony New Spain to Christianity. Priests arrived from Spain to spread the Roman Catholic religion. They had immediate success, helped by the Spaniards' complete military defeat of the Aztecs. To the Mexican people, the Spanish victories discredited both their old leaders and old gods. An Aztec poet expressed the feeling:

> We are crushed to the ground;
> we lie in ruins.
> There is nothing but grief and suffering...
> where once we saw beauty and valor.
>
> Have you grown weary of your servants?
> Are you angry with your servants,
> O Giver of Life?

The Spanish priests also built on similarities between Mexican religious traditions and Christian ones. The Aztecs, for example, had their own version of baptism and also used confession for the forgiveness of sins. The ceremonies of the Catholic faith appealed to the Mexicans' love of beauty, and many of the gods of the old religion were identified with the saints of Christianity. At the direction of the priests, Mexican laborers tore down temples and replaced them with churches, sometimes on the same sites as the pyramids where blood sacrifices had taken place. The very hill where Juan saw the Virgin had been sacred to the Aztec mother-goddess Tonantzin.

One of the most dedicated Spanish churchmen was a member of the Franciscan order, named Toribio de Benavente. The Aztecs called him Motolinia—"the Poor One"—because of his humble manner of dress. It was Motolinia who converted the solitary young Aztec and gave him the name Juan Diego at his baptism. From the time of his conversion Juan Diego became an ardent Catholic.

After his vision of the Virgin, Juan hurried to the Bishop of Mexico, Juan de Zumárragá. The bishop was proud of the success his priests had in converting the Mexicans. Earlier that year, he had written:

> We are very busy in the great task of converting the Indians.
> More than a million five hundred thousand of them have been
> baptized at the hands of our Franciscan fathers. Temples of

idols have been destroyed and more than twenty thousand idols ground to dust or burned.... Where formerly, in their infidelity, they are accustomed to sacrificing as many as twenty thousand human hearts, now they offer themselves not to evil spirits but to God.... Many of the converts fast and pray and discipline themselves with tears and sighings. Many of them know how to read and write and sing. They confess frequently and receive the holy sacrament with great devotion, and with joy preach the word of God to their parents....

The Spanish priests destroyed not only "idols." They systematically burned the libraries that contained the history and literature of the Mexicans. Among them were the books containing Nezahualcóyotl's poems. Only a few books survived.

Juan Diego, known for his piety, was welcomed by Bishop Zumárragá, who listened to his story. However the bishop was skeptical. He dismissed Juan with the words, "You will come again, my child, and I will listen to you more calmly. I will listen from the beginning and will think about the message you have brought."

Disappointed, Juan returned to the hill. He asked the Lady to pick a more distinguished messenger than himself— someone the bishop would believe. But the Virgin assured Juan that he was her choice. She asked him to return to the bishop and deliver her message again.

On the next Sunday, Juan met the bishop after Mass. Juan knelt and with tears in his eyes described his visions. Although the bishop listened patiently, he explained that he needed proof of such an extraordinary occurrence.

But Juan Diego's tale had piqued Bishop Zumárragá's curiosity. The bishop asked two assistants to follow the Aztec and report on what they saw. However, the assistants lost track of Juan after he left the city. When Juan reported the bishop's demand to the Virgin, she told Juan to come back the following day and she would give him proof.

But on Monday, Juan could not go to the hill. He was nursing an uncle who was sick from the plague. As his condition worsened, a doctor said that it was too late to save his uncle's life. Later that night, the uncle asked Juan to get a priest to prepare him for death.

When Juan left on Tuesday morning, he decided to go around the hill. He felt it was urgent to get a priest so his uncle could confess his sins before death. But the voice called him back and Juan turned to see the Virgin coming down the hill toward him. Juan explained why he could not stop and promised to return as soon as his errand was over. But the Virgin told him, "Let not your heart be troubled, be assured that he is cured." At that moment the Virgin appeared to Juan's uncle and cured him of his illness. This healing was the first miracle of the Virgin.

The Lady promised Juan a sign to give to the bishop. She asked him to climb to the top of the hill and pick flowers. It was wintertime, and nothing usually grew on the hill except a few weeds between the rocks. Instead Juan found beautiful roses and other flowers blooming. "My little one," said the Lady, "this bunch

of flowers is the proof and sign which you will take to the bishop." Juan picked the flowers and collected them in his cloak. The Lady touched the cloak and warned Juan not to open it until he was in the presence of the bishop.

As Juan waited to see the bishop at his palace, other petitioners admired the flowers sticking out of the cloak. They wondered where he had found them in December and asked Juan to open his mantle, but he refused. Finally, when the bishop received him, Juan unfolded his mantle and the flowers came tumbling out. But more amazingly, on the inside of the mantle was an image of the Virgin. The bishop fell on his knees at the sight of it. This was the second miracle of the Virgin.

The Virgin on the cloak had dark skin and her image soon became the most beloved religious symbol to the Indians in New Spain. The image was named for the Virgin of Guadelupe, who had been venerated in Spain. She was the patroness of Hernán Cortés and had appeared on his battle flag. Nevertheless, the Indians took the dark-skinned Madonna to their hearts. The news of her miracles caused more Indians to convert to Christianity. The "spiritual conquest" of Mexico would outlast the political rule of the Spaniards. Today Mexico is an almost entirely Catholic country.

As the Virgin had asked, a church was built on Tepeyac Hill. Almost at once it attracted pilgrims from all over Mexico. When Juan Diego died in 1548, he was buried there.

The Virgin of Guadelupe is today the patron saint of Mexico. The old church still stands, but a new cathedral was built alongside in 1976 to accommodate the enormous crowds that come to visit. Displayed behind the high altar is the miraculous cloak of Juan Diego, with the dark-skinned Virgin Mary's image still bright upon it.

Each year on December 12, Mexicans celebrate the feast day of the Virgin of Guadelupe. Thousands come from all over Mexico to crowd into the plaza in front of the church. Some make the final part of the journey on their knees, using spiny cactus leaves as pads. It is the most important religious shrine in Mexico and draws more pilgrims than any Catholic site in the world except Saint Peter's Basilica in Rome.

A Scamp's Life—
Diego de la Cruz

Sometime in the mid-1700s, Diego de la Cruz sat in the prison of the Holy Office in Mexico City. Diego was a slave of African descent who had been accused of blasphemy. Blasphemy, or the ridicule and contempt for the religious beliefs of the Roman Catholic Church, was a most serious crime in colonial Mexico. The Inquisition, another name for the Holy Office, was an agency of the Church, dedicated to rooting out any dissent from the True Faith. The Inquisitors were greatly feared, and anyone in Diego's position had good cause to worry.

Diego, however, regarded his arrest as an opportunity. He desperately wanted to free himself from a life of hard work and slavery. He came up with an extraordinary plan to fool the Inquisition and gain his freedom. The story of Diego de la Cruz gives an interesting picture of life in colonial Mexico for those at the bottom of society.

Diego de la Cruz was born in the city of Texcoco, the city that Nezahualcóyotl had once ruled. His mother was an African slave, but she was an ambitious woman who made money raising and selling poultry. She earned enough to buy her freedom from her master. Eventually, she purchased all her children from him as well, except for Diego. She left him in slavery to punish him, because he was always in trouble and disrespectful to his mother.

In the years after the Conquest, the Indians suffered a disaster of epic proportions. The Spanish brought with them smallpox, measles, chicken pox, and malaria. Because Mexicans had never been exposed to these diseases, a large part of the population died. Since we do not know the exact number of Mexicans at the time of Cortés' arrival, we do not know how great the disaster was. But by a conservative estimate, Mexico's population declined by 75 percent within a century of the Spanish Conquest.

For the Spaniards, this tragedy created a labor shortage. The Spaniards did not come to New Spain to work in mines or plantations. They came to gain wealth by living off the work of others. Because the Spaniards themselves shunned hard labor, they imported African slaves to their colonies in the New World to do this work.

Many Africans did not willingly suffer enslavement. Often they ran away from their masters. Escaped slaves were called *cimarrones*, or "untamed creatures," when they lived in the wilds of the countryside. Sometimes they formed bands to resist the government's attempts to capture them. A cimarrone named Yanga lived in the mountains for thirty years, leading a community of eighty African men, women, and children. When Spanish soldiers tried to wipe out Yanga's band, the Africans resisted for so long that the government eventually made peace with Yanga. He and his followers were officially freed.

In the larger towns and cities slaves might escape from their masters and hide in the poorer sections of the community. These escaped slaves became known as *leperos*, or lepers. Mexico City, grown to a population of over 100,000 in the mid-1700s, attracted many people who came seeking work. Outside the city center where the wealthy built their grand, luxuriously furnished homes, narrow streets held thousands of wooden shacks. Thieves, pickpockets, and the very poor struggled to eke out a living. Their life was hard and they had to look to their wits to survive. Diego de la Cruz is a good example of their kind.

Diego's first master in the city was a merchant named Juan de Gorostiaga. Hoping to earn money from Diego's labor, de Gorostiaga lent him to a tavern keeper. But at the tavern, Diego drank more than he worked. He also stole money from the tavern to gamble with. The tavern keeper presented Diego's owner with a bill for his slave's "amusements." De Gorostiaga was not amused, and decided to sell Diego to someone else.

Diego did not want to leave Mexico City. He enjoyed the city's taverns, crowds, and festivals. As the center of colonial Mexico, it was preferable to the plantations, mines, and little villages in the countryside. His mother, who may have been fond of him after all, advised him to marry a friend of hers, a free *mulatto* (a person part

Spanish and part African). Colonial law forbade masters to separate a slave from his free wife. Diego followed his mother's advice, and the merchant was forced to sell him to a resident of Mexico City.

Diego's new master was Pedro Belarde, an official of the colonial courts. Belarde wanted to use Diego as his coachman. But again Diego showed his skill for getting out of work. He drove the coach sloppily, weaving to the left and right, almost spilling his owner into the street. He frequently ran away, hiding in the back streets of the city for days. As punishment after being caught, he was flogged. Finally, Belarde gave up trying to control him and sold Diego to a priest.

Diego was twenty-two years old when Father Bartolomé de Balfermoso became his new master. The priest owned an *obraje*, or workshop, where cloth was made. He put Diego to work carding wool. In the obrajes of Mexico, workers toiled from dawn to dusk in hot airless conditions. Diego realized that he had jumped from the frying pan into the fire. This was the worst of his jobs.

At first Diego tried to cajole the priest into freeing him from the work. He pretended great piety, falling to his knees and saying the rosary aloud. Diego frequently asked the priest to hear his confession. Father Bartolomé was pleased and sent him to church. But on weekdays Diego was still stuck in the obraje. Although the workshop was heavily guarded, Diego managed to escape yet again.

When he was recaptured, the priest had him whipped. During the whipping Diego renounced his faith, called on the devil, and cursed the Virgin. Father Bartolomé was so shocked that he called a halt to the punishment.

Diego saw from this that he might be able to use blasphemy to his advantage. When he returned to the obraje, he told the other workers he was possessed by the devil. But all this brought him was separation from his fellow workers, so that he could not corrupt them.

When Diego escaped again, the priest told the Inquisition that his missing slave was a blaspheming heretic. Agents of the Inquisition soon found Diego. This time he was not returned to his master, but jailed on charges of blasphemy.

In jail, Diego came up with his amazing plan to gain freedom. He would not only admit to being a blasphemer but also claim to be a secret believer in Judaism. This serious admission would bring him to the attention of the highest officials of the Holy Office. Then he would say his self-accusations were false and describe his miserable life, winning their sympathy. He knew that only church officials at the highest level could grant freedom from enslavement.

In Spain, there was no freedom of religion. Everyone was required to be Roman Catholic. One of the Inquisition's chief duties was to check up on converted Jews to see that they were not secretly practicing their former faith. Those judged to be insufficiently devout could be forced to leave Spain. Even worse, some were tortured or killed.

The same rules applied in Mexico. Many Jews in Mexico were Portuguese who publicly adhered to the Christian faith. Portuguese had come to the Spanish colonies between 1580 and 1640, when

Spain and Portugal were united under one monarch.

The economic success of these Portuguese Jews aroused the jealousy of Christian businessmen. The Christians accused their Jewish rivals of secretly practicing their ancient faith. Now that the two countries were no longer united, the Portuguese Jews were also under suspicion as possible traitors.

In 1649 the Inquisition burned thirteen Jews at the stake in Mexico City as heretics. This form of execution had the gruesome name of *auto-da-fé*—meaning "act of faith." A huge crowd of people, wealthy citizens to lowly slaves, attended the public execution. Diego may have been among those who witnessed it, for it took place while he was still working for Father Bartolomé and pretending to be a pious Christian.

When Diego faced the Inquisition the following year, the hysteria of looking for Jews was at its height. The Inquisitors were astonished to hear Diego accuse himself of being "an observer of the law of Moses."

Diego told the Inquisitors an incredible tale. He claimed that on a Sunday holiday from the obraje he had met a free black friend, Pascual de Rosas. They decided to go into business selling clothes. Each put up money to buy clothes and rent a market stand. Diego claimed that Pascual told him that if they became Jewish, they would make more money.

So, Diego continued, he left the obraje the following Sunday to meet Pascual. Pascual told him that as Jews they must not eat on Sunday. They spent the afternoon in Alameda Park, watching the good-looking young mulatto women. In the evening Diego decided that he just had to eat. He and Pascual went to an inn where Diego knew the owner. She served them a meal and gave them a room for the night.

The clothing business proved less profitable than Diego expected. After a few days, Diego said, he was sorry to have become a Jew and wanted to be a Christian again. He went to his birthplace, Texcoco, and confessed his sins to a priest. The shocked priest said he could not absolve him. He turned Diego over to the Inquisition.

Only at a time when prejudice clouded all judgment could such a wild story be believed. The Inquisitors did what they were bound to do by law. They opened an official investigation of

Diego's report, and began to look for this heretic Pascual de Rosas.

De Rosas was nowhere to be found, nor had anyone else ever heard of him. The other workers at the obraje said that Diego had no money to open a clothing business. Sharper questions revealed that Diego had no knowledge at all of the beliefs of Judaism.

Diego then admitted the whole story was a lie and threw himself on the Inquisitors' mercy. He told them that he had always been a faithful Christian, but his miserable life as a slave had driven him to make up his story so that he would be brought before the Inquisition. He claimed that at the end of a workday he was "dead of fatigue and hunger." Father Bartolomé refused to allow him to spend time with his wife. He begged the Inquisitors to free him from slavery.

The Inquisitors were in a bind. They were embarrassed to have accepted such a ridiculous story and did not want to look foolish. So they swore Diego to secrecy. They warned him that if he ever revealed what happened, his punishment would be two hundred lashes and excommunication from the Catholic Church.

Father Bartolomé was brought before the court and ordered to pay for the costs of conducting the investigation and for Diego's food while in jail. The Inquisitors warned the priest not to punish Diego since he had already spent time in prison. Henceforth, the priest should allow Diego to visit his wife. The Inquisitors did not free Diego, but they gave his master some good advice: sell this troublesome slave as soon as he could.

The records of the Inquisition state that Father Bartolomé did as he was ordered. With that, Diego fades from history. We do not know whether he ever gained his freedom, but he probably had a smile on his face when he watched Father Bartolomé pay for his escapade.

Few records tell much of the lives of slaves like Diego or of the other Africans and Indians who labored in the mines and plantations, bringing riches to Spain and their Spanish masters. Only their names can be found in baptismal records or the dusty account books of slaveholders. Diego's life story tells us how much they yearned for freedom, and how far they would go to gain it.

Who bought Diego from Father Bartolomé? We do not know, but we can imagine that anyone who tried to enslave this free spirit would have taken on more than he bargained for.

"I, SOR JUANA"—
JUANA INÉS DE LA CRUZ

In 1664 thirteen-year-old Juana Inés de Asbaje waited to be received in the palace on the largest square in Mexico City. She was going to meet the beautiful Doña Leonor Carreto, wife of the viceroy of New Spain. The viceroy was the most powerful person in the colony. He was the personal representative of the king of Spain. As Juana waited, she realized that this meeting was an opportunity that could change her life.

Doña Leonor had arrived from Spain with her husband, the Marqués de Mancera, just a few months before. She was eager to attract the brightest and most amusing people to her court. A letter from Juana's relatives had piqued the Marquesa's curiosity. They described the girl as a treasure of learning who needed the protection of the viceregal court. When Doña Leonor inquired further, she learned that the girl was a young genius. That the girl was also poor, and her parents unmarried, did not disturb the Marquesa. It was enough that Juana was a *criolla*, a native of Mexico of Spanish descent, and that she was an intelligent young woman with poetic gifts.

Doña Leonor was enchanted with the beautiful young Juana. She saw a girl with long dark hair, fair skin, and large dark eyes. Her manner was refined, and she spoke well. The Marquesa determined to take Juana under her wing and invited her to live at the court. Juana became a lady-in-waiting and companion to Doña Leonor. Under her patronage, Juana was able to develop her talents, which would make her the greatest poet of colonial Mexico.

Juana was born near Mexico City in 1651. She came from the small village called Nepantla, or "the land in between," which overlooked two great snow-capped volcanoes. From a very early age, Juana had a great love of learning. She later wrote:

I was less than three years old when my mother sent an older sister to be taught reading at a school for small children.... Moved by sisterly affection and by a mischievous spirit, I followed her; and seeing her receive instruction, I formed such a strong desire to learn to read that I tried to deceive the schoolmistress, telling her that my mother wanted her to give me lessons. She did not believe me, since it was incredible; but to humor me she agreed. I continued to come and she to teach me, no longer in jest but in earnest: and I learned so quickly that I already knew how to read by the time my mother heard about the lessons from the teacher, who had kept them secret in order to break the pleasant news to her and receive her reward all at once. I had concealed it from my mother for fear that I would be whipped for acting without permission.

The idea of being whipped for wanting to learn seems strange to us today. But in colonial Mexico girls received little schooling. Their education stressed polite behavior and the skills of running a home. Subjects such as arithmetic, science, and literature were for men—who were believed to be superior to women in intelligence. Moreover, little girls had to be strictly obedient to their parents, just as later in life women had to obey their husbands.

Juana's curiosity though could not be suppressed. She never lost her desire for learning. It was so strong that when she heard that cheese made people slow-witted, she refused to eat it. She brought the same devotion to the study of Latin. If she did not meet her daily goal of memorizing a certain number of new words, she would cut off a few inches of her hair. "For it did not seem right to me," wrote Juana, "that a head so empty of knowledge, which is the most admirable adornment of all, should be crowned with hair."

Her greatest dream was to attend the university in Mexico City. Founded in 1551, it was the oldest in the New World—one of its founders was Bishop Zumárraga. Because it was open only to male students, Juana planned to dress as a boy and try to enroll. But her mother discouraged her.

The court of Doña Leonor would provide a second chance. Juana's talents blossomed in her new home. She met distinguished scholars and could read and discuss books with any of them. The viceroy was so proud of his young prodigy that he had Juana examined by professors from the university. They were amazed that someone so young, with little formal schooling, could answer their questions easily. In addition, she wrote poetry to celebrate happy occasions at court—birthdays, feasts, and public events.

She also wrote poems about love. One of her poems captures a universal problem:

> That Fabio does not love me, when I adore him
> Is an unequaled grief, and hurts my will;
> But that Silvio loves me, although I abhor him
> Is no less a penance, if a lesser ill.

Soon Juana had to make a choice about her future. Did she want to marry or enter a convent and be a nun? Those were the only choices open to young women. In colonial Mexico it was not possible for a woman to lead an independent life.

At age fifteen Juana made her decision. Later, she wrote that she chose the convent because "of my total disinclination to marriage." Though the obligations of a nun were "most repugnant to my temperament... it was the most becoming and proper condition that I could choose to ensure my salvation."

The confessor for the viceroy, Father Antonio Nuñez de Miranda, influenced her decision. Father Antonio was wary of women, seeing them only as temptations. He wrote as a guide for himself, "With all women I must show great caution, and not let them touch me, nor kiss my hand, nor should I look upon their faces or robes...nor seek friendship or correspondence with them. And I must close the door on all familiarity with women and be prepared to flee heaven and earth from them no matter how saintly they seem."

Nor did Father Antonio admire Juana's achievements and talents. He feared that her example would encourage other women to pursue literary and intellectual goals. Instead, Father Antonio encouraged Juana to abandon her pursuit of knowledge and work for the good of her soul.

He placed her in the Convent of the Barefoot Carmelites. She took the religious name Sor Juana Inés de la Cruz (Sister Juana Inés of the Cross), by which she is known today. The order of the Barefoot Carmelites was the strictest religious group in New Spain. The nuns' cells were sparse and cold and their food meager. At night, Juana's sleep was constantly broken by the necessity of getting up for prayer and religious services. Self-flagellation, or whipping oneself with a leather thong, was required daily. Juana's health broke under the strain. Three months after she entered the convent,

Doña Leonor brought her back to the court to recover.

Despite her bad experience Juana stood fast to her commitment to the Church. In February 1669 she entered the Convent of San Jeronimo in Mexico City. It was a pleasant change from the Barefoot Carmelites. Many convents, like this one, were comfortable places serving the unmarried daughters of the wealthy. The cells were pleasant rooms and the religious duties less strict. Moreover, she was allowed to receive visitors, and could still compose poems for the court. The Marquesa often came to see her, bringing gifts, candies, and sweetmeats.

Even so, Sor Juana had to struggle against her own nature. She saw this herself: "I thought that I had fled from myself, but—wretched me!—I brought myself with me and so brought my greatest enemy, that thirst for learning which Heaven gave me." No matter how much she tried to repress this thirst, "it would burst forth like gunpowder." The communal life of a nun was in conflict with her scholarly interests. Long after the other nuns had fallen on their beds from exhaustion, a candle still burned in Juana's cell. She was reading and writing.

Sor Juana strove to meet her obligations. She performed her religious duties and chores such as kitchen duty. She tried to be friendly and cheerful with the other sisters. Sometimes her patience was strained. One prioress (head of the convent) was especially dull-witted and got on Juana's nerves. Juana put up with her for as long as she could, but one day burst out with, "Be quiet, Mother, you're such a fool!" The mother superior was so offended that she reported Juana's words to the archbishop.

This time Juana was in luck, for he was an admirer of her accomplishments. The archbishop scribbled in the margin of the prioress' letter, "If the Mother Superior can prove the contrary, justice will be done." The matter was dropped.

In 1673 Juana was saddened to learn that the viceroy and his wife were returning to Spain. They had been like a family to Juana in the nine years since she had come to the court. Her sadness turned to grief when she heard that Doña Leonor had fallen ill only a few days after she left Mexico City and died. Juana composed poems to express her sadness:

> And love lament its bitter fate,
> For, if before, ambitious to enjoy your beauty,

It searched for eyes to see you,
Now those eyes serve only to weep.

Other visitors still came to see her at the convent. One of her best friends was Don Carlos Siguenza y Góngora, a fellow-spirit who shared Sor Juana's intense love of learning. As a young man, Don Carlos had entered the Jesuit order but in a dispute left that community. His first love was science, particularly astronomy, but he was also interested in geography, mathematics, ancient Mexican civilizations, and poetry.

The meetings between the two scholars in the reception rooms of San Jeronimo crackled with intellectual energy. Don Carlos brought Juana the latest scientific instruments from Europe. They discussed the new methods for observing and recording natural phenomena. Don Carlos praised Juana as one of the best poets and scholars of the age.

In 1682 a great comet appeared in the sky. Night after night people gathered to witness its progress across the heavens. With its long tail stretching behind, it was sometimes brighter than the

moon. The comet caused panic and fear, just as in Moctezuma's time. Even the priests felt that it was an omen of disasters to come.

Don Carlos and Sor Juana were among the few who realized that science could explain the frightening light in the sky. Don Carlos published a paper explaining that comets were natural phenomena that should be studied to learn more about the heavens. His paper was attacked by those who held superstitious beliefs. Sor Juana backed her friend. (A British astronomer on the other side of the Atlantic, Edmund Halley, watched the same comet and predicted the year of its return. When he was shown to be correct, the great comet was named after him. But that was seventy-six years later.)

Sor Juana also took up the cause of the rights of women, whose unequal treatment had always upset her sense of fairness. Particularly dear to her heart was the issue of women's education.

As in her childhood, there were still few schools in Mexico for girls. One reason was that women were not allowed to teach—and priests felt that it was improper for men to teach young women. Sor Juana asked, "What is wrong with allowing a mature woman, learned in letters and wholesome in conversation and habits, to take charge of of the education of young ladies?"

She even attacked the double standard for the sexes. Custom demanded that a woman remain a virgin till marriage, and then be strictly faithful to her husband, while the sexual affairs of men were winked at. She criticized men who sought to seduce women:

> Ignorant men who accuse
> Women wrongly...
> Why do you expect them to be virtuous
> When you encourage them to sin?

Sor Juana's poetry began to be published in Spain as well as Mexico and other countries. But her growing fame only fanned the jealousy of clergymen who thought her accomplishments were unholy and even unnatural. The bishop of Puebla led the attack. "Turn away from your scientific and worldly interests," he publicly warned Juana, "and devote yourself to holy activities as becomes a nun."

Juana was saddened. When she asked her friend Don Carlos for advice, he advised her to remain silent, warning that the Inquisition could be called to look into her affairs. Still, she chose to fight back. She published a letter defending a woman's right to pursue a scholarly career. Women had the same mental capabilities as men, she asserted. And she justified her poetry by pointing out that her gifts were God-given and should be used. The Bible itself, she pointed out, included poetry.

The exchange brought her old opponent, Father Antonio, into the argument. He had disapproved of Juana's success and fame. He warned that her salvation was at risk and played on her fear of dying without the grace of the Church. The strain took its toll on Sor Juana's health, and she gave in.

"I, Sor Juana Iñez de la Cruz, the worst in the world," she wrote in the convent book in her own blood. In her testament she promised to make a complete break with the past. She sold her library of 4,000 books and her musical and scientific instruments. Quietly she gave the proceeds to the poor of Mexico City. She spent days in confession with Father Antonio and promised to spend the rest of her life in repentance.

Her spirit broken, Sor Juana spent her last two years without writing. When a plague broke out in Mexico City in 1695, Sor Juana refused to leave the city, as many did to avoid the disease. Instead she stayed to nurse the nuns who had fallen ill. She left the convent to minister to the poor and sick within the city. Finally, she herself caught the disease and died.

Sor Juana's talents brought her little happiness in life. It was her sad fate to live at a time when a woman of intellectual gifts received scant praise or encouragement.

She never knew how much future generations would admire her work. Yet in the privacy of her cell, reading books and putting her own thoughts and feelings on paper, she felt the companionship of others she would never see. In her last poem, Juana teased her future readers:

> I am not who you think,
> Rather from afar you have given me
> Another being with your pens,
> Another breath with your lips.
>
> And different from myself,
> Among your poets I wander
> Not as I am, but instead
> As you imagine me to be.

C H A P T E R 7

THE GRITO OF DOLORES—
MIGUEL HIDALGO Y COSTILLA

In the early morning hours of September 16, 1810, a soldier galloped up to the house of Father Miguel Hidalgo. He had been riding all night to reach the town of Dolores, about 120 miles north of Mexico City. The soldier roused the priest to tell him alarming news: Their plot to overthrow the government had been discovered.

Father Hidalgo was part of a secret group that wanted to separate New Spain from Spain. They had planned to overturn the government of the *peninsulares*, or Spaniards, who enjoyed all the power and privilege in Mexico. Other members of the group were staying in Father Hidalgo's house. They had planned to raise the call for rebellion in December. But now, with their plot discovered, they decided to act at once. Father Hidalgo exclaimed: "Gentlemen, we are lost: the only thing we can do now is to seize the Gachupines!" (a nasty term for the Spaniards.)

They took up arms and marched to the town jail, where they forced the guards to free the prisoners. The local Spanish officials were rounded up and thrown into the cells.

Father Hidalgo rang the church bell, which brought people running from all over town. When his parishioners assembled in the church, Father Hidalgo climbed to the pulpit and began to address the crowd: "My children, will you be free? Will you make the effort to recover from the hated Spaniards the lands stolen from your forefathers three hundred years ago?"

His listeners, many of them mestizos and Indians, shouted their answer. "We will!"

"Mexicans!" Father Hidalgo called out, "Long live Mexico!" This speech—the most famous sermon in Mexican history—is remembered as the "Grito [cry] of Dolores." Hidalgo's call to action started the Mexican independence movement.

The man who gave that memorable speech was born on May 8, 1753, the second son of Cristobal Hidalgo y Costilla and Ana Maria Gallaga y Villasenor. His father was the *mayordomo*, or administrator, of a *hacienda*, one of the large farms and ranches that the Spaniards had built throughout Mexico. Miguel's ancestors had been in New Spain for a long time, and his surname, Hidalgo, indicates that his father's family descended from Spanish nobility.

The years Miguel spent growing up on the hacienda gave him a love of the people who worked the land. Yet his father wanted better things for his son. When Miguel was a teenager, his father sent him to Valladolid (today's Morelia) for further schooling. For the farmboy, city life was a heady experience, and Miguel enjoyed his studies at the College of San Nicolás Obispo. He gained a reputation as an expert debater that brought him the nickname El Zorro, or "the fox." When he received his degree, Miguel went to Mexico City to continue his education.

Afterward, he returned to San Nicolás as a teacher of Latin, the arts, and theology. At the same time he continued his religious studies with the dean of San Nicolás, who awarded Miguel a prize for two papers he wrote. The dean saw great promise for the young man, comparing him to "the industrious bee, which knows how to suck from flowers the most delicious honey. With the greatest joy in my heart, I foresee that you will become a light placed in a candlestick, or a city upon a hill."

Perhaps this prize advanced Miguel's academic career, for he was soon named rector of the college. But it was then that ugly rumors started to swirl about him. He was accused of giving his students books that conflicted with the teachings of Catholicism. The Inquisition sent a commissioner to investigate. Miguel's skills as a debater served him well, for he successfully defended himself against the charge.

In spite of any religious doubts he may have had, Miguel was ordained a priest. He left the college to serve in parishes in small rural areas. Even there, however, he did not escape the Inquisition's surveillance. He was called before the Holy Office to answer charges of heresy.

Hidalgo was accused of making statements that showed he did not believe in the virgin birth of Mary, that he was critical of the Pope, that did not believe in punishment by God, and that his sexual morals were questionable. Finally, he was charged with having read forbidden books. At this time, the French Revolution had broken out, spreading ideas of liberty and free thought. The Catholic Church regarded such ideas as dangerous, and had compiled a list of books that the faithful were forbidden to read.

Once more, however, "el Zorro" managed to refute all the charges against him. He escaped punishment.

In 1803, he succeeded his older brother as parish priest in Dolores. His parishioners included many Otomi Indians, and Father Hidalgo mastered their language so he could preach to them. He sympathized with the grinding poverty and discrimination that was their lot. Using his knowledge of agricultural methods, he encouraged the development of local industries to produce wine, honey, pottery, and even silk. But a law forbade unauthorized wine-making and silk manufacture, and when government officials visited the village, they ripped up the wine-grape vines and the mulberry trees on which silkworms fed.

Father Hidalgo opened his home to meetings of the local people, and formed a small orchestra to entertain his guests. The three lower classes of Mexican society—Indians, mestizos, and criollos—were all welcome at Father Hidalgo's parish house, and they began to discuss how to better their lives.

A favorite topic was politics. In New Spain, all the highest offices, in both government and church, were held by the peninsulares—people who had been born in Spain. No matter how talented a Mexican-born criollo was, he could not rise beyond a relatively low level. Father Hidalgo could not become a bishop; he was eligible only to hold the post of parish priest. As he watched less-talented Spaniards advance just because of their birthplace, he developed a strong dislike for these *gachupines*.

Father Hidalgo also joined a political club in the city of Querétaro. It was this group that had planned a rebellion for December of 1810. When the plot was discovered, quick action by the wife of one of the members had saved the day. When she learned that the plotters were to be arrested, she sent a messenger to warn him.

On the eve of the revolt, an eyewitness described Hidalgo:

He was of medium height, with stooping shoulders; his complexion was swarthy; his eyes were of a lively green color;...

and he was as white-headed and bald as though he had already passed sixty years of age. [He was actually 57.]… He was vigorous in his movements: a man of few words in ordinary conversation, when he entered into the heat of a dispute, after the fashion of a collegian, he became animated in his argumentation. He was not elegant in his dress, for he wore no other clothes than those which were ordinarily worn by the curates of small towns.

The costume of a village priest was a cloak or coat of black cloth, a sombrero, short pants and a woolen vest with a clerical collar.

That day, the crowd at the village church swelled with people arriving from the countryside. They armed themselves with machetes, knives, clubs, swords and a few muskets.

They set off for the village of San Miguel el Grande. As they marched, Father Hidalgo stopped at a church and took a banner of the Virgin of Guadelupe, the patron saint of Mexico. From then on, he carried it in triumph before him. The revered picture became the standard for Hidalgo's army. Their rallying cry was, "Long live religion! Long live our most Holy Mother of Guadelupe! Long live America! Down with the bad government!"

When Hidalgo's ragtag army entered San Miguel, the other plotters named Hidalgo as the military leader of the rebellion. More people joined his band as it moved on. When they reached the large town of Celaya, the mayor surrendered without a fight. As word spread of the rebellion, the Spanish viceroy condemned the followers of Hidalgo as "men deluded by false ideas." An old friend of Hidalgo's, Bishop Abad y Quiepo, denounced the rebel priest and his followers. The bishop excommunicated Hidalgo.

But Hidalgo ignored the condemnations. He led his untrained followers toward the city of Guanajuato. Guanajuato was set in a lovely valley surrounded by mountains with some of the richest silver mines in the colony. Workers from the mines left their jobs to join the fight. On September 28, Hidalgo demanded that the city surrender. The commander of its military garrison refused, and the rebels attacked.

The Spanish residents of the town hid themselves and their families inside a grain warehouse called the Alhóndiga de Granaditas. It was easily defended, and the first attacks by the rebels were beaten back. Then one of the miners, using a huge stone shield for protection, reached the Alhóndiga's entrance and set it afire. When the flames died down, the rebels swarmed into the building.

By this time Hidalgo's army had lost all discipline. Many Indians sought revenge for almost three hundred years of cruel mistreatment and the theft of their lands. Hidalgo's soldiers slaughtered most of the Spaniards within the Alhóndiga.

For the next two days Hidalgo watched helplessly as his army looted the town. "Guanajuato presents a most lamentable picture of disorder, ruin, and desolation," wrote an eyewitness. "The plaza and the streets were full of fragments of furniture, of the remains of merchandise which had been taken from the shops."

News of the fate of Guanajuato spread faster than Hidalgo's army. By the time Hidalgo reached the city of Valladolid, the colonial officials, called royalists, had fled the city. Valladolid was taken without any fighting. Here Father Hidalgo answered the charges of his critics. He proclaimed his faithfulness to Catholicism and called on Mexicans to stand together against the Spaniards. Hidalgo proposed a meeting of representatives from all over Mexico to make wise laws. He envisioned a government that would end poverty, promote the arts, and develop the industrial sector.

Hidalgo continued to gain followers. As he drew near to Mexico City, he commanded an army of about 80,000 people. A smaller royalist force waited on the Monte de las Cruces, a hill west of the capital. After fierce fighting, the Spaniards retreated, and Hidalgo's men cheered. The road to Mexico City lay open. The battle, however, had taken a heavy toll on the rebel forces and their ammunition was low. Hidalgo decided to retreat and regroup. It was a mistake; never again would he come so close to victory.

During the withdrawal, trained royalist forces attacked Hidalgo's army again. The battle, on November 6, went badly for the rebels and many of Hidalgo's men scattered into the countryside.

Hidalgo took the remnants of his force to Guadalajara. The city opened its gates to the rebels and welcomed them as liberators. Hidalgo sent a messenger to the United States to appeal for recognition of his cause, but the royalists captured the messenger. In Guadalajara, Hidalgo published a series of decrees. He declared an end to slavery, demanding that all slaves be freed within ten days on the pain of death to the slaveowners. He called for the return of Indian lands to the Indian community.

Hidalgo's decrees went too far for the majority of criollos. Although many criollos wanted to oust the peninsulares, they did not want a social revolution. Freeing the slaves and returning lands to the Indians would hurt the criollos economically. As a result, many of them went over to the side of the royalists.

At the beginning of the following year, a large royalist army appeared outside Guadalajara near the Calderón River. Ignacio Allende, one of the original plotters and a military officer, warned Hidalgo that an open battle was not wise. Instead, Allende suggested, the rebels should slip out of the town and carry on guerrilla warfare against the royalist forces. But Father Hidalgo believed that winning this fight was crucial. He faced the coming battle with confidence. The day before the fighting began, he boasted: "I go to breakfast at the bridge of the Calderón, to eat lunch in Querétaro, and to have dinner in Mexico City." With the banner of the Virgin of Guadalupe leading the way, Hidalgo's forces marched off to battle.

Although the royalist army was outnumbered, it was highly trained and well armed. The fight seesawed back and forth. But then a royalist cannon scored a direct hit on an ammunition dump, and a huge fire flared in the rebel camp. In the confusion that followed, the royalists attacked and routed the rebels. After the battle, Father Hidalgo was blamed for the defeat, and lost command of the troops. He fled north with his followers but was captured by a former rebel, now turned traitor.

In prison, Hidalgo refused to blame others. He proudly stated, "I placed myself at the head of the revolution."

But he did express regret for the death of innocent people. "Who will furnish water for my head and fountains of tears for my eyes? Who will cause to exude from the pores of my body the blood which flows through my veins in order that I may mourn day and night for those Mexicans who have died?"

The military leaders turned Hidalgo over to the bishop of Durango to be tried by the Church. He was publicly stripped of his clerical vestments and was condemned to be shot as a traitor. On July 30, 1811, he faced a firing squad. He blessed each of the soldiers before they shot him, telling them that one day Mexico would be free.

After the execution was carried out, Hidalgo's head was cut off and sent to Guanajuato. For ten years, it hung in a cage atop the Alhóndiga de Granaditas, in revenge for the slaughter that the rebels had carried out there.

Although Miguel Hidalgo's rebellion ended in failure, he lit a fire in the hearts of Mexicans that could not be extinguished. In 1821, ten years after his death, Mexico won its independence from Spain.

Hidalgo is revered in Mexico today as the Father of Independence. The bell that he rang to rouse his parishioners now hangs in the National Palace in Mexico City. Just before midnight on the eve of September 16, the president of Mexico tolls the bell to celebrate the Grito de Dolores. Mayors throughout the country call the people of towns and villages together to honor Father Hidalgo. Afterward, the merriment and fiestas begin and continue through the following day— Mexico's Independence Day.

C H A P T E R   8

VERY HOMELY BUT VERY GOOD—
BENITO JUÁREZ

In 1818 a barefoot boy walked down the dusty road to the city of Oaxaca. He was a twelve-year-old shepherd named Benito Juárez. While Benito was grazing his sheep that day, a group of mule drivers had told him about the wonders of the city. Benito was so entranced by their stories that he forgot to watch his flock. When he found one was missing, he dreaded telling his uncle. So he set out for Oaxaca, promising himself that one day he would repay his uncle for the lost sheep.

Benito was born in the tiny village of San Pedro Guelatao in the hills outside Oaxaca, in the southwest of Mexico. "My village was so small," he later wrote, "it had hardly twenty families." His parents were Zapotec Indians who died when he was three years old. An uncle took Benito in and raised him. The family was poor. Benito grew up in a mud hut where the meager food on the table was usually corn cakes.

In his village, Spanish was a foreign tongue—the people spoke only Zapotec. There was no school for the children. The few parents

who could afford to do so sent their children to Oaxaca for an education. Most children just continued to do what their parents had for generations. They needed no schooling to tend sheep or grow crops.

But Benito was different. Even as a young boy he had a burning ambition. "I became convinced that I could learn only by going to the city. I often urged my uncle to take me to Oaxaca. He did not do so." So when Benito saw his chance, he left. It was a journey of forty miles, but Benito was determined. One step at a time, he headed for the city where he would begin a new life. Someday, though no one knew it at the time, Benito Juárez would reach the pinnacle of power. He would become the most beloved figure in the country's political history and the only full-blooded Indian to be president of Mexico.

On Benito's arrival at Oaxaca, he searched for his older sister. He knew only that years earlier she had gone to the city to work for a wealthy family named Mazo. Somehow, he found the Mazo home, which was larger and more beautiful than any he had ever seen. He was too timid to knock at the front door. Instead, he went around to the back, where a small door led to the kitchen.

At first Maria Josefa did not recognize her brother because she had not seen him for so long. When Benito gave his name, she embraced him and persuaded the family to let him stay there temporarily.

Soon Benito met a bookbinder in the city, Don Antonio Salanueva. Salanueva was struck by the boy's intelligence. He offered to board Benito at his house, teach him Spanish, and send him to school. In return Benito made himself useful. He scrubbed the floors, ran errands, built the fire in the morning, washed dishes, and served Don Antonio's dinner.

Benito was an eager student and soon learned to read and write. Don Antonio encouraged him to continue. The Don hoped that Benito would become a priest. In the same year that Mexico became an independent country, the former shepherd started his training at a religious college. Benito enjoyed his studies, but felt no real call to the priesthood. When a law school opened in Oaxaca, he asked Don Antonio for permission to transfer to it. As a lawyer he felt he could help protect the rights of the Zapotecs and other

Indians within Mexico. His patron subsequently gave his approval.

During his years in law school, Juárez saw Antonio López de Santa Anna for the first time. General Santa Anna was to be honored at a dinner at the college. Juárez was chosen to be one of the students who waited on him. In later years the two men's paths would cross many times. Santa Anna would make himself president of Mexico nine different times. Benito Juárez would become a bitter enemy.

After Benito earned his law degree, he opened an office in Oaxaca. His years of study paid off, and he soon became successful. Juárez specialized in representing Indians, something few lawyers would do. A particular problem Indians encountered was the high fees that priests charged to perform religious rites such as marriages and funerals. Juárez once spent nine days in jail for bringing a parish priest to court for cheating an Indian. The Indians who came to him for help showed him how unjust Mexican society was toward the poor and downtrodden.

Juárez remained friendly with the Mazo family, who followed with pride the career of the man who had appeared footsore and hungry at their doorstep. One evening, Juárez came to Don Mazo and asked permission to marry his daughter Margarita. She was twenty years younger than Benito, and her father asked what she thought. "He is very homely," Margarita replied, "but very good." The couple married and remained devoted to each other for life. Their family grew to include twelve children.

Juárez's legal career showed him that to make a real difference he would have to enter politics. In 1845 he was elected to serve in the national legislature. The following year, war broke out between Mexico and the United States. General Santa Anna, who had earlier lost Texas, now seized the chance to redeem himself. He led his troops against an army from the United States. Once more, however, he was defeated. When United States troops occupied the Mexican capital, Santa Anna called for further resistance, but the Mexican government disowned him.

Fleeing south, Santa Anna tried to enter the state of Oaxaca. During the war, Juárez had become governor of his home state. Now he refused to give refuge to Santa Anna, earning the undying hatred of the general. Juárez' action, however, was popular with Oaxacans who were fed up with Santa Anna's corrupt regime.

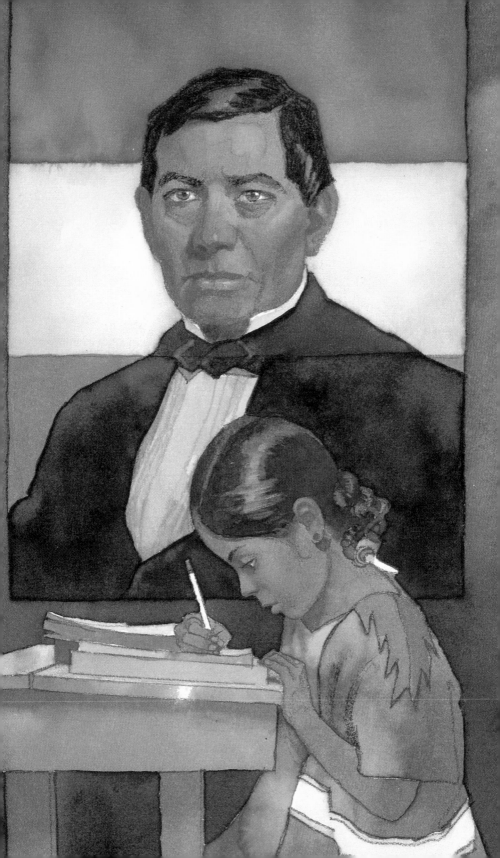

Juárez also won favor for his attempts to govern honestly. Determined to help his people, he built schools and made sure that tax revenues did not find their way into the pockets of officials.

Juárez was proud of his background. In his inaugural address for a second term, as governor, he said:

> I am a son of the people, and I shall not forget it; on the contrary, I shall uphold their rights. I shall take care that they become educated, that they lift themselves up, that they make a future for themselves, and that they abandon the life of disorder, vice, and misery to which they have been led by men who only with their words proclaim themselves their friends and liberators, but who by their acts show themselves to be the most cruel tyrants.

Five years later though, Santa Anna returned to power. He arrested Juárez and imprisoned him on San Ulloa Island in the Gulf of Mexico. Juárez escaped and fled to the United States, settling in New Orleans. To make ends meet, he made cigars and fished in the Mississippi River. Other political refugees from Mexico joined him.

The exiles asked each other: Why was Mexico so weak? The United States had gained almost half of Mexico's territory in the humiliating Treaty of Guadelupe Hidalgo that ended the United States-Mexican War. Yet military leaders continued to rule the country, enriching themselves and virtually ignoring the plight of the majority of Mexicans.

Juárez admired the United States' system of justice and government. He felt that for Mexico to thrive, it must have a strong constitution and a democratically elected government. He wanted a country where the Catholic Church and the army had less power. With the other exiles, he watched developments in Mexico and plotted to return.

Soon Juárez and his friends began to supply arms to guerrilla fighters in northern Mexico. In 1854, at the town of Ayutla, the rebels called for constitutional government. Mexicans rose up in rebellion and overthrew Santa Anna. The flamboyant dictator ended his days, forgotten and blind, in Cuba.

Juárez became the Minister of Justice in a reform government. He wrote a new law called the *Ley Juárez* (Juárez Law), which struck a blow for equal justice. It ended the legal privileges, called *fuero*, for the army and the clergy. Formerly, members of both groups had been tried only in special courts for any crimes that they committed. Now, for ordinary offenses, they would be tried in the same courts as the rest of the population. The military and clergy loudly protested, but Juárez was undaunted.

The next year the government took away the economic privileges of the Catholic Church, forcing it to give up its vast land holdings. The Church could keep only those lands on which churches or monasteries stood. These reforms were written into the Constitution of 1857.

Mexico's privileged classes did not give up power easily. The next year, civil war broke out between the reform government and its opponents. From their pulpits, priests called for the excommunication of members of the reform government. Pope Pius IX announced his opposition to the new Mexican constitution. The combined power of the army and the church was still strong, and the president of the reform government fled the country. Juárez, who was constitutionally next in line, took his place. Soldiers marched on Mexico City, forcing President Juárez to leave the capital. The military leaders took the city and proclaimed their own government.

Juárez retreated to Vera Cruz, a port city on the Gulf of Mexico. There he could get supplies from the United States, which still recognized him as the legal president. As the fighting seesawed back and forth, Juárez showed his mettle as a leader. On the surface, he did not appear to be an imposing person. Short and dark, he habitually wore only a plain black suit, contrasting with the elaborate uniforms of the generals. But he had great patience and inner strength and worked diligently and unselfishly for his goals. In the crisis, he remained courageous and imperturbable. On issues of principle, such as the repeal of the constitution, he refused to compromise. His determination inspired his followers.

In 1861 Juárez' followers won the so-called War of Reform. He re-entered Mexico City in triumph. He now faced the enormous task of rebuilding the country after three years of devastation. By the end of the year, however, he faced an even graver threat: invasion by France.

Napoleon III, the leader of France, wanted to control Mexico. French troops landed at Vera Cruz and headed for Mexico City. On May 5, 1862, an outnumbered band of Mexican soldiers stopped the

French advance. (This victory of Cinco de Mayo is celebrated as a national holiday today in Mexico.) But the French sent reinforcements, and their army drew nearer to the capital. Once more President Juárez prepared to abandon the city. Before he left, he watched as the Mexican flag was lowered from the staff in the square in front of the presidential palace. Juárez took the flag in his arms and kissed it. He shouted, "Viva Mexico!" and the crowd in the square took up the cheer. His message was clear: the capital might be occupied, but Mexico would not give up its independence.

Mexican conservatives welcomed the ouster of Juárez' government. They looked for a European ruler to act as a Mexican king with the support of French troops. When the conservatives asked Maximilian, brother of the Austrian emperor, to take the throne of Mexico, he agreed.

Maximilian was a weak, rather than a cruel, man, who tried to win the Mexicans' support. The lavish balls and concerts that he held with his wife Carlotta enticed many wealthy Mexicans to the capital. Moreover, Maximilian refused to overturn the Ley Juárez as many conservative supporters wanted him to. He offered Juárez a place in his government, but the president refused. Juárez remained near the border of the United States.

Juárez roamed the countryside in his famous black coach, rallying his followers. All the hopes of the downtrodden people of Mexico lay with the man in the coach. Wherever they could, Mexicans rose up in guerrilla warfare. The French troops put down pockets of rebellion savagely, only to face them again in other places. Both sides killed their captives, and the fighting became a bloody struggle to the death.

Juárez' position improved when former soldiers from both sides in the recently ended United States Civil War crossed the border to join his army. Slowly, Juárez' forces took back parts of Mexico. The president threatened supporters of Maximilian with the loss of their lands.

Napoleon III looked at the cost of the war and decided that the Mexican adventure was not worth the effort. He ordered the French troops to withdraw. Maximilian was secretly advised to abdicate and leave with them, but he chose to stay with his Mexican supporters. In 1867, when the last French troops left, Juárez' forces defeated Maximilian's army and captured the emperor. He was shot by a firing squad. After Empress Carlotta heard the news in Europe, where she was trying to win support for her husband's cause, she went insane.

Juárez' plain black coach rolled into Mexico City, greeted by cheering crowds along the route. For the rest of his life, he served as president. He continued his tireless efforts to create a society that would be fair to all. He decreased the size of the arm, and began to build schools throughout the country. It was his dream that no child would grow up without a chance at a good education.

In 1972, one hundred years after his death, Mexico celebrated the Year of Juárez to honor its most respected leader. Despite the years of violence and civil war, the defeat of the French had restored pride to Mexico. The Indians saw that one of their own could become president. Juárez' achievement gave the nation a sense of unity it had never before experienced.

Every Mexican school child today learns the story of his life, with its lesson that the humblest person can rise to greatness. He is honored for his devotion to the constitution and reform. "Let the people and the government respect the rights of all," Juárez wrote. "Among individuals as among nations, respect for the rights of others means peace."

C H A P T E R 9

"LAND AND LIBERTY"—
PANCHO VILLA AND
EMILIANO ZAPATA

On December 6, 1914, 50,000 ragged troops marched proudly into Mexico City. They belonged to two victorious armies whose leaders were about to meet for the first time.

Pancho Villa, a tall and heavy man, commanded the Army of the North. Emiliano Zapata, a slim figure on a white horse, led the Army of the South. Mexico was in the midst of a violent revolution that had been going on for four years, and would last for another six. More than a million people died in the decade between 1910 and 1920. In a sense, it was the final stage of the revolution that Father Hidalgo had begun. At long last, peasants and Indians had risen up to take their land from the rich.

Villa and Zapata, the two most charismatic leaders of the revolution, met at Xochimilco, once the site of the Aztecs' floating gardens. Eyewitnesses described the contrasts between the two men:

> Villa was tall and robust, weighing at least 180 pounds, with a florid complexion. He wore a tropical helmet after the English style…. He was clad in a heavy, brown woolen sweater, which was loosely woven, with a large rolled collar… khaki military trousers, army leggings and heavy riding boots. Zapata…was much more the Indian of the two. His skin was very dark, and in comparison with Villa's his face was thin with high cheek bones. He wore an immense sombrero, which at times hid his eyes.

The conference began awkwardly. Both men preferred action and fighting to talk. But when the conversation turned to their mutual enemy, Venustiano Carranza, their words, "like tinder, burst aflame." Each man described his personal hatred of the "First Chief," who, like them, was originally a revolutionary leader.

Villa said of the people who followed Carranza: "Those are men who have always slept on soft pillows. How could they ever be friends of the people, who have spent their whole lives in nothing but suffering?"

Zapata agreed: "They have always been the scourge of the people.... Those cabrones! [billy-goats] As soon as they see a little chance, well, they want to take advantage of it and line their own pockets! Well to hell with them!"

Between them, the two men had forced Carranza and his followers to flee Mexico City. Now, Villa took great pleasure in sitting in the president's chair. Zapata, on the other hand, wanted nothing to do with presidents and palaces. "I want to die a slave to principles, not to men," he said. This was the only time that Villa and Zapata ever met, and it marked the high point of their power. More bloodshed was to follow.

The man who became Pancho Villa was born Doroteo Arango in the northern state of Durango in 1878. His parents were sharecroppers on a large hacienda. Doroteo was a rebellious child, always in trouble. He refused to go to school and served time in prison for theft. When he was seventeen, his sister was raped by a wealthy landowner. Doroteo lay in wait with a rusty rifle and killed the man. Captured, he was sentenced to death, but he escaped from prison and changed his name to Pancho Villa, after an outlaw ancestor.

Villa began a life on the run, taking work as a miner and as a vaquero. Eventually, he joined a gang of cattle rustlers and became their leader. When government troops pursued him, he crossed over into the United States. He joined the United States army and served with Theodore Roosevelt and his Rough Riders in Cuba. Though he had no schooling, he had a keen intelligence, and the experience of combat taught him military tactics.

In Mexico, Porfirio Díaz had governed for more than thirty years. His rule brought prosperity to a small elite group of wealthy Mexicans and the many foreigners who invested in Mexico. For the vast majority of the Mexican people, conditions were grim. More and more of the land was concentrated in a few hands; most Mexicans were living on the edge of starvation as sharecroppers or poorly paid *peons*, or farm laborers.

In 1910 Porfirio Díaz looked forward to re-election to his sixth term as president. He planned a great celebration to mark the centennial of Father Hidalgo's Grito of Dolores. But in April, Halley's comet flashed across the Mexican sky. Just as in the time of Moctezuma, many Mexicans saw it as an omen of death and destruction.

That same month, Díaz learned that he would have an opponent in the election: Francisco Madero. Throughout the country, political clubs sprang up in support of Madero. Díaz reacted by arresting Madero and rigging the election. After the Grito celebrations were over, he released Madero from jail.

Madero fled north and called for the overthrow of Díaz. The response was electric, setting off an insurrection in the northern state of Chihuahua. Guerrilla bands of farmers and peons attacked towns and haciendas. News of the revolt set off more outbreaks of violence in the south.

By this time, Pancho Villa had returned from the United States. He joined the rebels and soon attracted a large group of followers. On May 20, 1911, his troops took the city of Juárez.

Ten days later Cuernavaca, an important city south of the capital, fell to another rebel army. Its leader was Emiliano Zapata. Zapata was born in 1877 in the southern state of Morelos. A mestizo, he worked as a child with his father on their small farm. After his father died, Zapata became the sole support of his mother and three sisters. He loved riding horses, and saved enough money to buy himself a fancy saddle. All over the region hacenderos, or ranch-owners, hearing of his skill, asked him to train their horses.

One day a rich hacendero asked Zapata to take charge of his stable of horses in the capital. The job paid well and Zapata agreed. But when he saw the luxury of the stables, with marble tiles lining the stalls, he was infuriated. How could people treat their horses so well when in the countryside peons lived in huts made of straw and adobe? He quit the job, returned to Morelos, and started to work to improve the lot of the villagers.

Morelos was sugar hacienda country. Over the years, the large landowners had taken away much of the Indian communal land, called *ejido*. The Indians had formerly farmed the ejido as a group. The hacenderos planted sugarcane on it and gave the Indians a few meager plots to scrape out a living. In 1909 a group of villagers who were trying to regain their land elected Zapata as their leader.

When the landlords and local government refused to deal with him, Zapata organized the villagers into armed bands. After Madero's call for Díaz' overthrow brought an outbreak of fighting in the north, Zapata decided the time was ripe to seize the land by force.

Although loosely organized, Zapata's Army of the South was effective. Zapata's rallying cry, "Land and Liberty," aroused the deepest desires of the landless peasants. The Zapatistas fought guerrilla-style with hit-and-run raids. Because the majority of the people backed their cause, they could find hiding places everywhere.

Zapata's words thrilled his followers. "Seek justice," he said, "not with your hands, but with a rifle in your hands." Moreover Zapata's program was clear enough for everyone to understand— take back the land. Land to grow their own corn and land to participate in the cycle of nature just as their ancestors had. The *milpa*, or cornfield, was the center of Indian spiritual life because it was the source of food that the ancient gods provided.

Zapata often made his speeches to the villagers in Nahuatl rather than Spanish. A teen-aged girl recalled the day when the Zapatistas arrived in her village:

> All his men wore white clothes: white shirts, white pants, and huaraches [Mexican sandals].... Señor Zapata went to the front of his men and spoke to all of the people of Milpa Alta.
>
> Join me [he said].... I rose up in arms and I bring my countrymen. We no longer wish that our Father Díaz watch over us. We want a much better president. Rise up with us because we don't like what the rich men pay us. It is not enough for us to eat and dress ourselves. I also want everyone to have a piece of land so that he can plant and harvest corn, beans, and other crops. What do you say? Are you going to join us?

After the cities of Juárez and Cuernavaca fell, President Díaz saw the handwriting on the wall. He agreed to leave the country. But he had a warning for his successor: "Madero has unleashed a tiger, now let us see if he can control it."

The new leader would see the truth of this remark when he arrived in Mexico City. Waiting for him was Zapata. Their meeting was dramatic. Zapata wore a large black sombrero and held his carbine in hand. He pointed to the gold watch on Madero's vest.

"Look, Señor Madero," Zapata said, "if I, taking advantage of being armed, steal your watch and keep it, and then we meet again sometime and you are armed, wouldn't you have the right to demand that I return it?"

Somewhat embarrassed, Madero agreed that was so. "Well," Zapata continued, "this is exactly what has happened to us in Morelos where some of the hacendados have forcibly taken over the village lands. My soldiers, the armed peasants, demand that I tell you respectfully that they want their lands returned immediately."

Zapata's blunt talk did not sway Madero, who was a hacienda owner himself. He asked Zapata to give him time. Madero's main concern was to establish democratic procedures for Mexico so that free elections could be held.

Zapata soon lost patience. At the end of the year, he broke with Madero and proclaimed his Plan of Ayala. It called for the immediate return of land stolen by landlords and corrupt officials. He also demanded that large landholders turn over one-third of their land to the poor. Zapata gathered his forces again.

In the north, Madero's hesitant policies also caused discontent. Villa began to reorganize his rebel troops, but he was captured and jailed. Madero ordered that he not be executed. In his jail cell, Villa passed the time learning how to read.

Meanwhile, in the capital, people were restless and unhappy with Madero. But there the opposition was led by supporters of the former dictator, Díaz. They wanted Madero to take stronger action against the rebels. Early in 1913 Madero was brutally murdered by Victoriano Huerta, one of his own generals. His death ushered in the most violent phase of the revolution.

Throughout Mexico, fighting erupted between the *federales* (government soldiers) and rebel bands. The flames of burning haciendas lit up the skies as the marauders looted and killed. In the south, the Zapatista revolt spread from the state of Morelos to the states of Guerrero, Pueblo, Tlaxcala, and Mexico. Huerta declared himself president, but he had little power outside the capital. The whole country was aflame with revolution.

The rebel movement had no central command. Local groups formed their own bands as small as a few dozen or as large as a few hundred. Attacking wherever they could, they often took their weapons from the enemies they killed. No quarter was given. Prisoners were simply lined up against the wall and shot. Women *soldadas* fought beside the men, and often led their own groups. Following the troops were *soldaderas*, women who nursed the wounded and buried the dead.

The governor of a northern state, Venustiano Carranza, tried to form an organized resistance to Huerta's government. He named himself First Chief and called his army the Constitutionalists. Villa joined his forces to Carranza's cause and was rewarded by being named a general.

Pancho Villa became a legendary figure, beloved even by those who had never seen him. His violent nature and frequent womanizing—he reputedly had twelve wives—made him a symbol of machismo. An American reporter described the man: "He looks rather gentle, except for his eyes, which are never still; they are full of energy and brutality."

Villa's troops adored him, following wherever he led. They galloped on horseback all over northern Mexico, terrorizing their enemies. Long afterward, a Villa follower recalled:

> We learned to ride like hell, to eat when we had food, and to sing when there was none. When we had to move fast and silently, we shifted from horse to horse at a gallop. We thought Pancho knew the roads by smell. Many of our men were killed, but others took their place again and again. But how we loved Pancho Villa!

Carranza soon found that Villa was an unreliable ally. No one could control or command this free spirit. He took his troops wherever he pleased, attacking when he chose to, without any thought for an overall military plan. Moreover, Carranza feared Villa's growing popularity. When Villa led his men toward Mexico City in 1914, Carranza sent another general, Álvaro Obregón, to take the city before Villa arrived. Huerta fled to the United States, leaving Carranza as First Chief.

As you have read earlier, however, Villa and Zapata united against him. Throughout the Mexican Revolution, generals and their armies frequently changed sides. The people called them *generales de dedo*, or "finger generals," because you had to count them on your fingers to keep them straight. Almost all of the revolutionary leaders met violent deaths.

Villa himself was chased out of the capital at the beginning of 1915. Carranza sent Obregón after him to destroy Villa's power once and for all. When the two armies met at Celayo, Villa made a mistake. He was best at hit-and-run fighting, but here he committed his army to a full-scale battle. Obregón's powerful artillery tore Villa's forces to pieces before they could come within rifle range.

Villa was defeated, but not destroyed. He retreated back to the north with the remnants of his army. Angered that the United States president, Woodrow Wilson, had recognized Carranza as president of Mexico, Villa took on "the colossus of the north." His troops crossed the border into New Mexico and shot up the town of Columbus.

This was too much for Wilson, who sent General John Pershing with the United States Army against him. But Villa led Pershing's troops on a wild goose chase, trapping them in a series of ambushes. In less than a year Pershing withdrew without capturing Villa. The escapade only added to Villa's renown and glory.

Venustiano Carranza wanted to cement his power by establishing a regular government. He called together a convention to write a new constitution. The Constitution of 1917 established a political system with a congress, supreme court, and president. But the president was forbidden to succeed himself, to avoid having a dictator like Porfirio Díaz. The constitution called for the return of Indian lands. Workers were guaranteed a six-day work week and the right to organize and strike.

Carranza was not pleased with the constitution. He felt it was too radical. But he accepted it, stating that it set goals that would be reached in the future. He wanted to gain support for finishing off his remaining enemies.

For the last two years, Carranza's troops had been pounding away at the strongholds of the Zapatistas in the south. Despite widespread destruction of the haciendas and farms, and the loss of some troops, Zapata had managed to keep his force together. He openly challenged Carranza, claiming that he had betrayed the revolution. In a public letter addressed to Citizen Carranza, Zapata declared: "You turned the struggle to your own advantage and that of your friends who helped you rise and then shared the booty—riches, honors, businesses, banquets, sumptuous feasts..." He ended by saying the people were "mocked in their hopes."

Carranza knew that Zapata had to go. But Zapata was crafty, not easy to trick. The scheme agreed on was to draw Zapata into an ambush. A colonel named Jesús Guajardo pretended to defect from the national troops. He offered to bring his group of five hundred armed men over to Zapata's side. In order to make his offer credible, Guajardo captured a town and killed over fifty federal officers.

Zapata agreed to a meeting on April 10, 1919. As he stepped forward to greet Guajardo, Zapata was cut down in a hail of bullets.

The death of Zapata is remembered each April 10 by Mexico's agriculture minister at Cuantla. He lays a wreath at the martyr's statue and promises more land reform. The promises are needed, for many of Mexico's people are still poor and landless.

Carranza did not long survive Zapata. When it became clear that he intended to make himself dictator, another rebellion arose and Carranza was killed. Villa's old enemy, General Obregón, became the new president.

To end the fighting, Obregón offered Villa amnesty and granted him a large hacienda. Villa retired to a life of ease there. Many of his former soldiers became vaqueros on the hacienda. Three years later though, assassins shot Villa as he was driving his car.

Pancho Villa remained celebrated in legend even after death. He was described as the only person to invade the United States. Though some called him an outlaw, he was a Robin Hood to many Mexicans. A well-known saying sums up his popularity: "Villa was hated by thousands, but beloved by millions."

CHAPTER 10

THE ELEPHANT AND THE DOVE—
DIEGO RIVERA AND FRIDA KAHLO

In 1922, Diego Rivera stood on a scaffold painting a mural in the Preparatoria, a school in Mexico City. The thirty-six-year-old painter was one of the most famous artists in the world. His physical appearance was enough to call attention to himself. He was incredibly fat, weighing more than three hundred pounds, and his eyes bulged out of his head like a frog's. His clothes reflected his love of attention. On his head sat a large sombrero, and on his feet were black miners' boots. His wide belt barely held together the baggy shirt and trousers that looked like they had been slept in.

Rivera was the most famous of many muralists working in Mexico in the 1920s. Throughout the country, walls and ceilings—whole buildings—blossomed with the bold pictures they painted.

The Mexican Revolution had unleashed a wave of national pride. President Álvaro Obregón and his education minister, José Vasconselos, encouraged the development of a true Mexican style in the arts. The revolution had elevated the mestizo and Indian to a new dignity. Vasconselos spoke of Mexico as gifted with a "cosmic race"—a mixture of white, Indian, and African.

Artists began to glorify this new view of Mexico. Since the ten years of fighting had destroyed many buildings, new ones were built. Rivera and the other artists looked at the new, blank walls and saw them waiting for an art that was too great in spirit for ordinary canvases.

Rivera loved the public attention that his fame brought him. He talked animatedly as he worked on his mural that would cover 1,000 square feet of wall in the auditorium. Often he brought girlfriends to keep him company as he worked.

A seventeen-year-old prankster at the Preparatoria captured Rivera's attention. She stole food from his lunch basket and soaped

the stairway that led from the room. But Rivera had a peculiar way of walking—his step was carefully measured—and he did not slip. To her friends, the girl whispered that she had fallen in love.

Flying into the auditorium one day, she called to the artist working high above. He agreed to let her watch him paint. He later described her:

> She was dressed like any other high school student but her manner immediately set her apart. She had unusual dignity and self-assurance, and there was a strange fire in her eyes…. A year later I learned that… her name was Frida Kahlo. But I had no idea that she would one day be my wife.

Diego Rivera showed his artistic talent at a very early age. Born in the silver mining town of Guanajuato in 1886, he was the son of middle-class parents. Although he liked to claim that he combined all parts of the "cosmic race," Diego's ancestors were really European. His father was a rural school inspector who encouraged his son's desire to paint. From the age of three, Diego began to cover the walls of the Rivera home with his drawings.

The family moved to Mexico City in the 1890s so that Diego could develop his talent. He enrolled in the San Carlos Academy to study painting. But the academy taught its students how to imitate old-fashioned European styles. Diego found little joy in copying European landscapes at the academy. He was more interested in the folk art that he saw on the streets of the city. The patterns in Indian pottery and blankets dazzled him.

A government grant enabled Diego to continue his artistic studies in Europe. In Paris he became part of the generation of young artists who were experimenting with new styles. The young Spanish artist Pablo Picasso made a deep impression on Rivera. He also got involved in radical politics and became an admirer of the Russian Revolution of 1917.

Rivera kept abreast of developments in Mexico and strongly supported the revolution. In 1915 he painted a portrait of Emiliano Zapata. Indeed, throughout his career, Zapata would be Rivera's most frequent subject.

When Rivera returned to Mexico in 1921, he saw his homeland through new eyes:

> It was as if I was reborn, reborn into a new world. All the colors I saw seemed sublime; they were clearer, richer, better, more

filled with light. The black tones had a depth which they never attained in Europe. I was in the very center of the world... where colors and forms existed in absolute purity. In each and every thing I saw a potential masterpiece—the masses of people, the marketplaces, the fiestas, the battalions on the march, the laborers in the workshops and fields—in each splendid face, in each luminous child. I was convinced that even if I lived a hundred lifetimes I would never exhaust the storehouse of buoyant beauty.

Rivera shared his enthusiasm with the education minister, Vasconselos, who took him on a trip through Yucatán. Rivera was awed by the sight of the Mayan ruins and did extensive sketches of them. He was excited by the idea of creating public art on walls where everyone could see it. From the trip came the commission to paint a mural at the Preparatoria.

In 1923 Rivera started on his first masterpiece. For the Ministry of Education building he created 124 murals that lined the courtyard and patio. This mammoth work, illustrating the different lives of Mexicans, took the artist four years of almost superhuman labor. Rivera painted from eight to fifteen hours a day. He worked like a man possessed, taking only short breaks for food. Sometimes he had tacos brought to him on the scaffolding so that he could eat as he worked.

Soon Frida Kahlo reappeared in Rivera's life. She was the daughter of a Mexican woman and a German-Jewish immigrant. Her father earned his living as a photographer. Frida's happy childhood was interrupted when she caught polio and had to spend a year in bed. The disease left her with one shrunken leg, but she refused to let it keep her from an active life.

Frida had a lively intelligence and excelled at school. Her academic ability got her into the Preparatoria, where she first saw Diego. But her carefree school career came to a halt in a freak accident in 1925. When she and a friend were riding home on a bus, an electric trolley plowed into it. Frida was impaled on a steel handrail and suffered injuries to her spine, ribs, collarbone, and foot.

The accident was the most traumatic event of her life. At first she hovered near death, then began another long, painful convalescence. For the rest of her life, Frida faced many operations and continual physical pain.

While recovering at home, she painted her first self-portrait.

She presented it to the friend who had been with her on the day of the accident. This started a pattern for Frida. She painted countless pictures of herself, always giving them to friends almost as if she feared they would forget her without them. Painting became her way of expressing friendship and dealing with the pain that she lived with.

In 1928 Frida met Diego again. When she showed him her paintings, he found them interesting and different. Soon a courtship began and the following year they were married. Frida's mother thought the petite Frida and the heavy six-foot-tall Diego an odd couple. She dubbed them the elephant and the dove.

Their marriage was stormy, even from their wedding day. As Frida recalled the event:

> Diego went on such a terrifying drunken binge with tequila that he took out his pistol, he broke a man's little finger, and broke other things. Then we had a fight, and I left crying and went home. A few days passed and Diego came to fetch me.

Diego now began the largest project of his life. He was offered the task of decorating the National Palace. For his theme, he took the entire epic story of Mexico itself. But it was history seen through the unique eye of Diego Rivera.

The mural was divided into three parts. The first showed the original people of Mexico in their battles, culture, myths, and legends. The second showed the cruel conquest by the Spaniards and the Mexicans' struggle for independence through the 1910 revolution. In the third part Diego painted his dream of Mexico's future. He showed a socialist paradise, with happy workers at their machines. Diego lavished more than nine years on this great work.

He was now a famous artist, whose reputation had spread to the United States. Thinking that Rivera would separate his art from his politics, rich business leaders asked him to create murals for their buildings.

He and Frida left for the United States. He painted a mural for the San Francisco Stock Exchange and then went on to Detroit. Edsel Ford, son of the billionaire carmaker Henry Ford, wanted Rivera to paint a mural for the Detroit Institute of Arts.

Edsel Ford may have regretted his choice of artists. The mural shows gangs of workers, resembling faceless robots in goggles and masks, building cars at giant machines. A crowd of wealthy, frowning men and women watches from the background. But the mural remained as Diego painted it.

However, his next work created a scandal. The Rockefeller family asked him to create a mural for Rockefeller Center, then under construction in New York City. Crowds formed to watch the heavy-set artist climb the scaffolding each day to work on his huge creation. Rivera painted the Soviet Communist leader V. I. Lenin into the mural. This was unacceptable to the richest capitalist family in the United States. Diego was asked to remove Lenin, and he refused. Rivera was fired and the mural was painted over.

The couple returned to Mexico City, where they built two studios for themselves, connected by a bridge. While Diego worked on an epic scale, Frida excelled in miniature painting. Frida became interested in traditional Mexican *exvoto* paintings. These were works that gave thanks to a saint, the Madonna, or Christ for a blessing performed on the artist's behalf. Often they showed a limb that was healed or a person who had recovered from an illness. Frida began to create her own exvoto paintings to depict her suffering and pain.

Rivera brought home a colorful, long, ruffled dress worn by the women of Tehuantepec. It appealed to her interest in the Indian traditions of Mexico. She later adopted this kind of dress for everyday wear. The dress hid Frida's deformed leg and was also a political statement. The women of Tehuantepec were reputed to be strong and beautiful. Their society traditionally had been run by women.

The marriage of two such strong-willed people was sometimes unhappy. It might have been different if they had children, but Frida's accident made that impossible. Her pregnancies ended in miscarriages. There is no doubt that Frida desperately wanted a child. She kept a large collection of dolls and dollhouses in her bedroom. She even had a birth certificate for one of the dolls and treated them as lovingly as real babies.

Living with a man like Rivera would have been difficult for anyone. He was like a force of nature, giving in to his desires without consideration for others. He was often unfaithful to her. The two divorced in 1939 but then remarried the following year on a trip to San Francisco. Their attraction for each other was stronger than their disagreements.

Rivera was a man of tremendous artistic energy, which did not flag as he grew to middle age. When he had no murals to work on, he painted portraits of the famous to earn money that he needed for other projects. He generously encouraged younger artists.

In the 1940s, he formed two great new plans. One was to recreate the city of Tenochtitlán as it stood before the Spanish Conquest. Halls were set aside in the National Palace for Rivera to rebuild the ancient Aztec city. His other dream was to build a pyramid like the ones erected before the Conquest. On land that Frida owned, he started building. The projects were unfinished at his death.

Rivera's last great mural was *Sunday at Alameda*. To create it he drew on memories of his youth. During the time of Porfirio Díaz, he had often visited Alameda Park with his parents. The mural recreates the pleasures of the park along with historical events that took place there. Through the picture stroll upper-class people in their finery, *charros* in their flamboyant outfits, and peddlers hawking tacos, candies, and balloons. The vast mural, fifty feet long, includes President Benito Juárez and his enemy General Santa Anna, Maximilian, Porfirio Díaz, and Francisco Madero. Camping out on the grass are the Yankees who invaded Mexico's capital in 1848 and the troops of Zapata and Villa who arrived in 1914.

In the midst of this grand panorama of history walks a fat little boy with a frog sticking out of his pocket. Certainly, this is Rivera's recreation of himself. And because he was now an old man, he painted the boy holding the hand of a skeleton, wearing a scarf made of corn sheaves. At either end of the scarf are a snake's head and fangs. The death-figure resembles the ancient Mexican goddess of death, still celebrated each year on the Day of the Dead. Part of the Mexican spirit is a fatalistic attitude toward death—it will come soon enough, so why not laugh at it? On the Day of the Dead, people exchange candies and toys shaped into skulls and skeletons. So Diego showed himself happily clasping death's hand among the scenes of boyhood.

In this last mural, Diego did not forget his wife Frida. She stands behind the fat boy and the skeleton, holding a little sphere with the Chinese symbol of yin and yang on it. Yin and yang—the two opposing forces, masculine and feminine, in the universe. In his lifetime, the passionate Diego Rivera had encountered only one spirit equal to his. Without her, he could not live.

Frida's health was failing while Diego worked on his last mural. Often, she could not rise from her bed. In 1953, to lift her spirits, Diego arranged the first public exhibition of her works. On the day it opened, Frida arrived on a stretcher in an ambulance. The admirers of her work swarmed around to congratulate her. It was one of her life's happiest moments. The following year she died. The last entry in her diary reads, "I hope the exit is joyful— and I hope never to come back."

Frida's family home is today a museum devoted to her art. It contains her collection of folk art along with her dearest possessions, the dolls. Mexicans and foreign visitors alike flock to it each year to share her spirit. Though she lived in her husband's shadow, her own reputation as an artist has grown after her death. Today she is as famous as Diego. All the little paintings she gave away to friends are now treasured works of art.

A friend of the couple described the effect of Frida's death on Diego: "He became an old man in a few hours, pale and ugly." Still, Diego continued to paint for another three years even as his vigor failed him. Toward the end he began to lose the power to move his right arm and complained, "The brush no longer obeys me."

Diego Rivera was one of the great artists of modern times. His brush brought life and color to the epic of Mexican civilization. The sheer amount of his work is staggering—literally miles of it is displayed on walls throughout Mexico and the United States. His legacy is reflected on the buildings of modern Mexico City. It is impossible to imagine Mexico's capital today without the imaginative genius of Diego Rivera.

"I WANT TO DANCE"— AMALIA HERNÁNDEZ

"Papa, I want to dance. May I learn how to dance?" asked Amalia Hernández. The eight-year-old girl was sitting in the living room of a thirty-room town house in Mexico City in the mid-1920s. Her father, Don Lamberto Hernández, was a wealthy businessman who owned a large ranch and was also a senator. As a father, he took the traditional view of the role of women. He had worked to amass a fortune in order to raise the social position of the family. Daughters of the wealthy did not perform in public. His attitude was shared by Amalia's mother, Doña Amalia Navarro, who was a teacher.

But Don Lamberto was also an indulgent papa. He agreed that Amalia could learn to dance "if you do it only at home, never show your legs, and dance only for me and your uncles." Don Lamberto built a special dance studio near the Hernández home. He invited some of the greatest teachers in the world of dance to come and teach Amalia. One teacher had danced with Anna Pavlova, the greatest ballerina of the time. Another had danced for the Paris Opera.

Amalia was thrilled with her lessons, and she showed great talent. To her parents she presented a sunny face and kept within the limitations they had set. Still within herself, she kept the secret wish: to dance on the stage in Mexico City. It was a dream that never left her.

As Amalia studied traditional ballet, her dream took a different turn. She found that neither classical music nor its formal steps had the same appeal for her as Mexican music and dance. From childhood, Amalia loved the folk songs from Chihuahua that her mother taught her to play on the guitar. Visiting her father's ranch in the state of Tamaulipas, she watched with fascination and then memorized the songs and dances of the workers celebrating the sugar harvest. On a holiday in Vera Cruz she watched musicians pluck their homemade harps and miniature guitars with the speed of a hummingbird's wings. At a feast, she watched the traditional wedding dance, the *bamba*, with its fast steps and graceful movements.

Amalia was thrilled by the variety and color of Mexico's folk art. Hidden away in the mountains and plains of the country was a vast treasure house of talent. She decided that her life's work should be to bring Mexico's rich and varied traditions to the public. She would take these folk dances and transform them into ballets that would be presented on the concert stages of the world.

It was a long time before Amalia could realize her dream. Amalia obediently did what her mother wanted—take piano lessons and prepare to be a teacher. At night she took business courses to please her father. In her few moments of free time, she studied Mexico's history and folklore. Yet her dream never left her mind.

Her father wanted to protect his daughter from what he saw as the dangers of the stage. When one of Amalia's teachers suggested that she come to rehearsals to work, he exclaimed, "Work? I have fixed it so that no daughter of mine will ever have to work!" Amalia remained silent but told herself, "I will not argue. I will just go ahead and do!" That became her motto. But Don Lamberto cut off her allowance and hid her jewels to keep her from selling them to pay for outside lessons.

Amalia retaliated by enrolling in the Campesina, a free government program for teaching dance to poor farmers. She dressed in shabby clothes and wore dark glasses so that no one would recognize her. For several months she attended classes until her father discovered her ruse. He sent a chauffeured limousine to pick up his disobedient daughter.

Amalia struck out on her own again. When she was twenty-three, she landed a job as a dancer in a Mexican movie. One day the director was shooting a scene in the Zócala, the main square in Mexico City. Amalia was dancing in a chorus line and the cameras were rolling. Suddenly a squad of motorcycles approached with sirens blaring. Behind them was the official limousine of the Mayor

of Mexico City, Don Lamberto Hernández. Glaring at his daughter, he ended her movie career.

Amalia's rebelliousness took its toll in her personal life. At the age of seventeen, she had married Rafael Lopez, a young lawyer. But Amalia's career hopes made a regular married life difficult. She had a daughter, but the marriage soon ended in divorce. Two more daughters followed from three other unsuccessful marriages in the next twenty years. "My husband is the ballet," remarked Amalia.

To be involved in dance, Amalia took a job for $30 a month at the Institute of Fine Arts as a teacher and choreographer, or designer of dances. The Institute was sponsored by the government and its troupe performed at the Palace of Fine Arts.

Amalia realized one of her wishes as she danced at this national theater. Mexico's greatest composer, Carlos Chavez, created the *Sinfonia India*, a new ballet based on Mexican music. She swirled across the stage in one of the starring roles. At last she stood in the footlights, basking in the cheers of a real audience. When Amalia suggested new dances based on Mexico's folk tradition, however, she was told that they did not "belong" at the Palace of Fine Arts.

When she was thirty-four, Amalia made her hardest decision. She quit the Institute of Fine Arts to strike out on her own. Taking some of her best students, she formed her own dance company. "One must fulfill oneself," she said.

She sold her house and jewels to raise money. She also pawned one of her father's cars, presenting him with the ticket that would allow him to redeem it. She explained that he would not miss it—he had so many cars!

Don Lamberto threw up his hands. If Amalia was really so determined, there was no sense in opposing her. Secretly, he admired his daughter's spunk. He offered to help her financially.

Even so, the year 1952 was hard. Amalia Hernández struggled to create new dances for the company while performing herself. Then, the following year, a television station asked her company to do a weekly show. This was an enormous task for Amalia. She had to create, rehearse, and direct a brand-new ballet each week.

Fortunately, the show captured the attention of the Mexican Department of Tourism. It decided to send Amalia's troupe abroad as an official representative of the country. Amalia did not know how people in other countries would respond to her new style of dance. She was dancing now not only for herself, but also for Mexico.

After her small troupe performed at the Festival of the Pacific in Los Angeles in 1958, she waited to see what the newspaper critics would say. The next morning, she read the glowing reviews with pride. The following year, she scored another success in Chicago.

The president of Mexico heard about the honors that Amalia's troupe had brought to Mexico. He ordered the government to give her company its full support. For the first time Amalia had enough money to pay dancers, musicians, choreographers, and set designers. And she had another offer that probably brought a smile of triumph. The Institute of Fine Arts asked her to come back to create for Mexico "the finest ballet in the world."

Amalia worked like a demon. She traveled the country to look for talented musicians and dancers, gathering new sources for her own inspiration. With a tape recorder and photographer, she visited country fairs, fiestas, ranches, and even little night clubs. Amalia found talented people everywhere. One of her leading dancers was a Yaqui Indian whom she found in an orphanage in Sonora. Amalia often set out with an empty bus, returning to Mexico City with a full load of dancers to be auditioned.

Amalia called her troupe the Ballet Folklórico. She brought groups of dancers from all over Mexico to perform in the capital. Performers in six-foot-high headdresses played Quetzal, the god-bird. Yaqui Indians performed the ancient deer dance of their people. A joyful wedding dance from Tehuapacán was recreated on the stage of the Folklórico. For the first time, the people of Mexico City saw the treasures of their country's cultural history.

Amalia used musical instruments from the time of Moctezuma, such as the *huechetl*, or seashell war horn. Its moaning sound fascinated audiences. The flute-like *chirima* of the Aztecs was followed by the sound of guitars and trumpets of a *mariachi* band from Jalisco. The Ballet Folklórico offered its audiences an opportunity to enjoy the treasures of Mexico's varied cultural heritage.

Because her troupe was sponsored by the government, officials sometimes thought they could give orders to Amalia. Few tried to do so twice. The pride of the Palace of Fine Arts was its immense glass Tiffany curtain. When a government official told the

85

Ballet Folklórico's director that she could not raise the curtain without the permission of the production manager, Amalia was furious. "If that curtain doesn't go up in five seconds," she yelled, "I'll kick my foot right through it!" The curtain—all twenty-two tons of it—went up right away.

Amalia became world-famous in 1961. In that year, she took the Ballet Folklórico to Paris for the Festival of Nations. The Festival was like a cultural Olympics for dance. Amalia's dancers would compete with the finest troupes from Russia, China, India, and Ghana.

On May 9 Amalia waited nervously in the wings of the Sarah Bernhardt Theater. She had created a performance that would retell Mexico's history. The house lights went down and she led her troupe on stage. As the curtain rose, Amalia was center stage in the costume of an Aztec priestess. She beat out slow rhythms on the Aztec battle drum, the *teponaxtle*. Once more Moctezuma ascended his throne, four centuries after the last Aztec ruler had died.

Then the beat of the music grew faster, following the tempo of a Spanish dance. Mestizo girls, their colorful skirts spinning outward, whirled around the stage with handsome men in Spanish jackets and trousers.

Shots rang out, and the stage filled with soldiers and soldadas, wearing ammunition belts and sombreros and carrying carbines. They sang the revolutionary songs, called *corridas*, so dear to the

Mexican heart. Amalia reappeared on stage, dancing the role of one of the revolution's soldada heroines, Juana Gallo.

For the finale, the company performed a dance created by Amalia: *Christmas in Jalisco*. All the color and wonder of Mexico's culture was on display, to the lively music of a mariachi band. The dancers formed a circle to perform the *Jarabe Tapio*, or Mexican Hat Dance. As the music came to a smashing climax, streamers fell from the ceiling. The audience rose to its feet, shouting and applauding. The cheers went on for minutes, as Amalia and her dancers stood in the footlights, almost dazed by the reaction.

Word of the performance spread through Paris, and people rushed to buy tickets for another show. The Ballet had to move to a larger theater to hold the crowds. The judges of the Festival of Nations awarded the Ballet Folklórico first prize.

After that, Amalia's troupe was in demand everywhere. The Ballet Folklórico made several world tours, winning the praise of critics and the popularity of audiences. The style that Amalia had created appealed to many people who had never seen a classical ballet. She showed that the music and dance of Mexicans could be transformed into an art form that was the equal of any in the world.

Amalia used her fame and wealth to set up schools to teach Mexican children the art of the dance. One of them was in the Hernández mansion, where Amalia first performed for her family, dreaming of larger audiences. The worldwide fame of the Ballet Folklórico prompted her to form several more dance companies; some are on tour overseas while others remain at home. Foreign performances of the Ballet Folklórico bring to the rest of the world a portrait of Mexico's magnificent cultural heritage.

More recently, Amalia's daughter, Norma López Hernández, has taken over some of Amalia's duties in administering the business details of the troupe. Amalia's brother, an architect, designed a building to house a dance school, TV and film facilities, and a theater for a children's troupe. Amalia wants to make sure that any child who wants to dance can have the opportunity to learn.

Every Sunday morning, her troupe performs in the Palace of Fine Arts. The Quetzal bird lives again. The rich history and culture of Mexico comes to life in the art that Amalia has created. The girl who wanted to dance has made her dream a reality that enriches the world.

GLOSSARY

Auto-da-fé: "Act of Faith," or the execution by fire of heretics.

Bamba: The traditional Mexican wedding dance.

Caciques: Chiefs and leaders of Indian societies.

Calmecac: A special school for the children of the Aztec and Texcoco nobility.

Casco: The headquarters of a large hacienda or latifundia.

Charro: A particularly skilled Mexican cowboy.

Chocalatl: A drink made from cocoa beans, honey, vanilla beans, and spices mixed in hot water.

Cimarrone: An escaped slave who lived in the wilds.

Corrida: A folk song or ballad.

Criolla (female) or **Criollo** (male): Mexican-born person of Spanish descent.

Ejido: The land on which the Native Mexicans lived and farmed. Traditionally, it was the property of the entire group, and they shared the farm work among themselves. Rich landowners took much of it for their haciendas. One of the goals of the 1910 Revolution was to restore the ejido to the Native Mexicans, or Indians.

Federales: The government troops during the 1910 Revolution.

Fuero: The special privileges that the clergy and military enjoyed before the reform law of Benito Juarez.

Gachupines: A derogatory term for the Peninsulares.

Great Speaker: The Aztec ruler.

Grito de Dolores: The "Cry of Dolores," the sermon given by Father Miguel Hidalgo on September 16, 1810, in which he called Mexicans to revolt against the Spanish colonial government. The anniversary is celebrated as Mexico's Independence Day.

Hacendado: An owner of a hacienda.

Hacienda: A large plantation, estate, or ranch.

Holy Office: The Inquisition.

Inquisition: An agency of the Roman Catholic Church dedicated to rooting out any dissent from Catholicism.

Lepero: An escaped slave who lived in the city slums.

Ley Juarez: The "Juarez Law," introduced by Benito Juarez when he was Minister of Justice. It curbed the special privileges of the clergy and the military.

Machismo: Manliness, a highly respected value in Mexican society.

Malinchism: The practice of preferring foreign things to Mexican things, referring to Malinche, the Indian woman who helped Cortez conquer the Aztec empire.

Mayordomo: The administrator of a hacienda.

Mestizo: A person of mixed Spanish and Indian ancestry.

Mulatto: A person of mixed Spanish and African ancestry.

Obraje: A workshop.

Peninsulares: People living in Mexico who were born in Spain. In colonial Mexico, they were at the top of society.

Peon: A worker on a hacienda. Because by law the peons were bound to their hacienda, they were much like slaves.

Presidio: A fort.

Royalists: Those who backed the Spanish king in the Mexican wars of independence.

Soldada: A woman revolutionary soldier.

Soldadera: A woman who served as a helper for the revolutionary soldiers.

Tithe: A type of tax that required farmers to set aside part of their crops for the government.

Vaquero: A cowboy.

Viceroy of New Spain: The chief representative of the Spanish king in the Americas.

BIBLIOGRAPHY

Bailey, Bernardine, *Famous Latin-American Liberators*, New York: Dodd, Mead & Co., 1964.

Bailey, Helen Miller, and Grijalva, Maria Celia, *Fifteen Famous Latin-Americans*, Englewood Cliffs, NJ: Prentice-Hall, 1971.

Bernal, Ignacio, *Mexico Before Cortez: Art, History, and Legend*, Garden City, NY: Doubleday Anchor Books, 1973.

Bray, Warwick, *Everyday Life of the Aztecs*, New York: Peter Bedrick Books, 1968.

Burland, C.A., *Montezuma, Lord of the Aztecs*, New York: Putnam's, 1973.

Cadenhead, Ivie E., *Benito Juarez*, New York: Twayne Publishers, 1973.

Calderón de la Barca, Frances, *Life in Mexico*, New York: Everyman's Library, 1970.

Davies, Nigel, *The Aztecs: A History*, Norman, OK: University of Oklahoma Press, 1980.

Davis, Harold E., *Makers of Democracy in Latin America*, New York: Cooper Square Publishers, 1968.

Fehrenbach, T.R., *Fire and Blood: A History of Mexico*, New York: Collier Books, 1973.

Gillmor, Frances, *Flute of the Smoking Mirror*, Albuquerque, NM: University of New Mexico Press, 1949.

Gillmor, Frances, *The King Danced in the Marketplace*, Tucson, AZ: University of Arizona Press, 1964.

Henderson, James D., and Henderson, Linda, *The Notable Women of Latin America*, Chicago: Nelson-Hall, 1978.

Hergera, Hayden, *Frida: A Biography of Frida Kahlo*, New York: Harper and Row, 1983.

Kandell, Jonathan, *La Capital: The Biography of Mexico City*, New York: Random House, 1988.

Keen, Benjamin, ed., *Readings in Latin American Civilization*, Boston: Houghton Mifflin, 1955.

Leon-Portilla, Miguel, ed., *The Broken Spears: The Aztec Account of the Conquest*, Boston: Beacon Press, 1962.

Martí, Samuel, *The Virgin of Guadalupe and Juan Diego*, Mexico City: Ediciones Euroamericanos, 1973.

Meyer, Karl E., *Teotihuacán*, New York: Newsweek Books, 1978.

Meyer, Michael C., and Sherman, William L., *The Course of Mexican History*, New York: Oxford University Press, 1979.

Miller, Kal, and García-Oropeza, Guillermo, *Mexico*, Hong Kong: Apa Productions, 1983

Miller, Robert Ryal, *Mexico: A History*, Norman, OK: University of Oklahoma Press, 1985.

Millon, Robert P., *Zapata: The Ideology of a Peasant Revolutionary*, New York: International Publishers, 1969.

Milton, Joyce, *The Feathered Serpent and the Cross*, New York: HBJ Press, 1980.

Padden, R.C., *The Hummingbird and the Hawk: Conquest and Sovereignty in the Valley of Mexico, 1503-1541*, New York: Harper Torchbooks, 1970.

Rankin, Allen, "Because Amalia Wanted to Dance," *Theatre Arts Magazine*, October, 1963.

Reavis, Dick J., *Conversation with Moctezuma*, New York: William Morrow and Co., 1990.

Reed, John, *Insurgent Mexico*, New York: International Publishers, 1969.

Riding, Alan, *Distant Neighbors: A Portrait of the Mexicans*, New York: Knopf, 1985.

Robertson, William Spence, *Rise of the Spanish-American Republics*, New York: The Free Press, 1946.

Roeder, Ralph, *Juarez and His Mexico*, New York: Viking, 1947.

Soustelle, Jacques, *Daily Life of the Aztecs*, Stanford, CA: Stanford University Press, 1962.

Stuart, Gene S., *The Mighty Aztecs*, Washington, D.C.: National Geographic Society, 1981.

Wolfe, Bertram D., *The Fabulous Life of Diego Rivera*, New York: Stein and Day, 1963.

Wohl, Gary, and Ruibal, Carmen Cadilla, *Hispanic Personalities*, New York: Regents Publishing Co., 1978.

Womack, John, Jr., *Zapata and the Mexican Revolution*, New York: Vintage Books, 1968.

S O U R C E S

Introduction: The Eagle and the Cactus
page 4: Huitzilopochtli's messages, Davies, Nigel, The Aztecs, pp. 7, 10.
page 5: Octavio Paz quoted in Meyer, Karl E., Teotihuacán, p. 22.

Chapter 1: Nezahualcóyotl
page 6: "My dearly loved son... "Stuart, Gene S., The Mighty Aztecs, pp. 81-82
page 8: "Here you see the house... " Gillmor, Frances, Flute of the Smoking Mirror, p. 17.
page 9: "Out of your cotton... " Ibid., p. 18.
page 9: "It seems as if... " Davies, op. cit., p. 74.
page 10: "He was a pious man... " Stuart, op. cit., p. 83.
page 11: "My flowers shall not cease... " Bray, Warwick, Everyday Life of the Aztecs, p. 52.
page 12: "God, our Lord... " Stuart, op. cit., p. 82.
page 12: "I Nezahualcóyotl, ask myself," Davies, op. cit., p. 117.

Chapter 2: Moctezuma II
page 17: "I have seen with utmost certainty... " Padden, R.C., The Hummingbird and the Hawk, p. 101.
page 17: "O Lord of all creation...." Davies, op. cit., p. 234.
pages 17-18: "The stags came forward... " Leon-Portilla, Miguel, The Broken Spears, p. ix.
page 18: "Moctezuma descended from his litter... " Riding, Alan, Distant Neighbors, pp. 82-83.

Chapter 3: Malinche
page 24: "Broken spears lie in the roads;... " Meyer, Karl E., op. cit., p. 145.

Chapter 4: Juan Diego
Account of Juan's visions: Martí', Samuel, The Virgin of Guadelupe and Juan Diego.
page 29: "We are crushed to the ground;... " Meyer, Karl E., op. cit., p. 145.
pages 29-30: "We are very busy in the great task... " Miller, Robert Ryal, Mexico: A History, pp. 144-45.

Chapter 5: Diego de la Cruz
Diego's "confession": Kandell, Jonathan, La Capital: The Biography of Mexico City.

Chapter 6: Juana Inés de la Cruz
page 41: "I was less than three... " Keen, Benjamin, Readings in Latin American Civilization, p. 163.

page 42: "That Fabio does not love me... " Kandell, Jonathan, op. cit., p. 224.

page 42: "With all women I must show great caution... " Ibid., p. 223.

page 44: "I thought that I had fled from myself... " Keen, op. cit., p. 163.

pages 44-45: "And love lament its bitter fate... " Henderson, James D. and Linda, Ten Notable Women of Latin America, p. 82.

page 46: "Ignorant men who accuse... " Ibid., p. 91.

page 47: "I am not who you think... " Ibid, p. 95.

Chapter 7: Miguel Hidalgo y Costilla
Account of Father Hidalgo's sermon: Riding, Alan, op. cit., pp. 32-33.

pages 51-52: "He was of medium height... " Robertson, William Spence, Rise of the Spanish-American Republics, p. 88.

page 53: "Guanajuato presents a most lamentable picture... " Ibid., p. 96.

page 55: "I placed myself at the head of the revolution... " Ibid., p. 106.

Chapter 8: Benito Juárez
page 60: "I am a son of the people... " Cadenhead, Ivie E., Benito Juarez, p. 35.

page 63: "Let the people and the government... " Ibid., p. 123.

Chapter 9: Pancho Villa and Emiliano Zapata
page 64: "Villa was tall and robust... " Meyer, Michael C. and Sherman, William L., The Course of Mexican History, p. 537.

page 68: "All his men wore white clothes... " Ibid., pp. 507-08.

page 69: "Look, Señor Madero... " Ibid., p. 508.

page 70: "We learned to ride like hell... " Wohl, Gary and Ruibal, Carmen Cadilla, Hispanic Personalities, p. 164.

Chapter 10: Diego Rivera and Frida Kahlo
page 75: "She was dressed like any other... " Hergera, Hayden, Frida: A Biography of Frida Kahlo, p. 33.

pages 75-76: "It was if I was reborn... " Kandell, Jonathan, op. cit., pp. 446-47.

page 77: "Diego went on such a terrifying... " Hergera, Hayden, op. cit., p. 100.

Chapter 11: Amalia Hernández
Conversation between Amalia and her father: Rankin, Allen, "Because Amalia Wanted to Dance."

INDEX